When Agile Gets Physical

HOW TO USE AGILE PRINCIPLES TO ACCELERATE THE DEVELOPMENT OF PHYSICAL PRODUCTS

Katherine Radeka and Kathy Iberle

Chesapeake Research Press
Camas, Washington, USA

Table of Contents

Table of Figures

A Note About Agile

Throughout this book, we use the term "agile" the way our community of hardware developers uses it. For them, Agile (with a capital "A") is Agile Software Development, by which they usually mean either Scrum or SAFe®. We're well aware that these are not the only two variants of Agile Software Development, but they are the ones we encounter nearly 100 percent of the time when we're working with physical product teams, and the ones most often pushed onto these teams by Agile coaches who lack experience with physical products. So, we capitalize Agile every time we're referring to the body of *practices* and *tools* developed to help software teams become faster, more flexible and more responsive.

These choices won't be satisfying for some Agile experts. Engaging in debates around Agile Software Development practices and tools would lead to a very different book. Instead, our primary focus here is on the principles of agile (with a lowercase "a"). It's those agile principles that create the conditions for increased agility, regardless of context. We'll apply those principles to the specific problems that physical product developers encounter so that they can optimize their workflows to realize the same promises of agility: speed, flexibility and responsiveness.

The Right Framework for the Job

The seed for this book was planted in a frustrating conversation with an Agile Software Development expert. He claimed to be working to adapt Agile for physical products — but that wasn't what he was actually doing. He was arguing that organizations didn't need — and didn't want — more than one framework for project management. They should *Just. Use. Agile.*

He had set up time to meet with us because he knew that Katherine's work, embodied in the Rapid Learning Cycles framework, was a proven solution for adapting agile principles to the early stages of physical product development. But it became clear early in the conversation that he was too attached to the terminology and tools of his own flavor of Agile Software Development, and he didn't have enough grounding in the principles that make Agile work.

He also didn't know that since 2015, Katherine had been called in on a series of "Agile Rescue Missions." She had helped untangle hardware teams that had become so bound up in misguided applications of Agile Software Development methods that their projects had come to a grinding halt. Katherine saw common patterns among these teams: backlogs that had blown up all out of proportion to the project, too much time spent trying to manage their backlogs, and teams losing track of the overall plan to deliver the product. Even worse, Agile methods were not solving

1

the problems that led to products that took too long, cost too much or delivered disappointing results.

Katherine guided these teams towards methods that used agile principles to solve these specific problems. This book will share how these teams learned to use smaller batches of work, fast feedback loops and other agile principles to accelerate the flow of work through hardware development. To do that, she had to focus them away from blindly applying practices and tools developed to solve a different set of problems in a different domain.

These Experiences Felt All Too Familiar

These conversations felt like many Katherine had about Lean ten years ago, when the field of Lean Product Development was flooded with people from Lean Manufacturing who gave out bad advice to Development teams. A lot of time, money and life energy was spent on programs that did not move the needle on performance — at all.

Today we have a lot of people from the Agile Software Development world who are making the same mistakes that the Lean Manufacturing experts made about Lean Product Development. In fact, we've had clients — and prospective clients — tell us that they were told "We can't use Rapid Learning Cycles because we have to use Agile." Whenever we hear this, we know that the organization is following Agile practices and tools but doesn't really understand why they work. If they did, they'd know why that statement doesn't make sense.

It's Not Just Rapid Learning Cycles

Any practice or tool that is not on the approved list of Agile tools — especially if they were used in the past to support waterfall development — is at risk of being put on the "not Agile" list of tools to avoid. If you don't know the principles behind Agile, then you don't know why Agile practices and tools work. If you don't know why those work, then any change to them threatens your ability to deliver benefits from Agile.

We've encountered many advocates for Agile, including many consultants and coaches, who treat Agile like it's a religion, one with rituals that must be adhered to strictly, beliefs that cannot be questioned, and strong boundaries to protect the Agile teams from outside influences that would dilute the team's use of Agile practices and tools. Such advocates have confused the rituals and beliefs with the principles behind them. When they expand Agile into new spaces, they bring the rituals, beliefs, practices, and tools — but not the principles.

They've fallen victim to the Law of the Instrument.

The Law of the Instrument

Most of us have heard some form of the expression "If you have a hammer, everything is a nail." It's been around since at least the 1800s. The first documented use comes from Abraham Kaplan, an expert on research methods in the 1950s and 1960s, who often said, "Give a small boy a hammer, and he will find that everything he encounters needs pounding." He called this the Law of the Instrument. Psychologist Abraham Maslow refined this to "If all you have is a hammer, everything looks like a nail."

The Law of the Instrument applies to business processes and methodologies especially well. Consultants and thought leaders are particularly prone to this error because we make money by selling our expertise. It's natural for any business to look for opportunities to grow their markets and expand their influence. This is a cognitive trap.

The Law of the Instrument Is a Cognitive Trap

Katherine has been deeply engaged with two communities where the Law of the Instrument has been triggered: the Lean community and the Agile community. They both have in common a set of principles that are sound and broadly applicable. Lean is focused on eliminating waste through better problem-solving. Agile focuses on continuous delivery of value in a flexible structure that accommodates change. They actually have common roots in applying insights from queueing theory (reduce batch sizes), using standard work for repetitive tasks and empowered, self-organizing teams. They even share the concept of a daily standup meeting.

Every area of a business has waste, and every area benefits from continuously delivering value. So, it's no surprise that Lean started in manufacturing but has always seen itself as a comprehensive enterprise management system that should be used everywhere. Agile started in software development but now sees itself as an enterprise management system that should be used everywhere. At the level of principles, both methodologies are on solid ground. The problem is at the level of practices and especially the tools.

Same Principles — Different Practices and Tools

In general, we know that continuous flow is better than big batches. We see lots of examples of this in both the physical world and the virtual world. In Lean, this is the principle of One Piece Flow. In Agile, this is the continuous delivery of value by organizing work into small iterations.

Lean practices and tools that support One Piece Flow include kanban systems to coordinate upstream and downstream processes, value stream maps to highlight waste, and rapid tool changeovers. Agile practices to support the continuous delivery of value include sprints, Sprint Planning and Demo Events, test-first development and daily builds. Agile tools like kanban boards and automated regression testing support these practices.

You'll note that "kanban" overlaps here, although the term is used differently based on context. This is not a coincidence. This is what happens when you try to bring a tool from one problem domain into the other: It gets adapted so heavily that it loses its original meaning. Even though the concept originated at Toyota, a line worker would have a hard time recognizing what a software team calls a "kanban" and has never seen a kanban board. The thing they have in common is the principle of continuous delivery/One Piece Flow. (We'll cover this example in-depth in Chapter Two.)

In Agile, we're seeing the same thing happen with "user story" and "demo." When you take the practice or tool out of context, it has to be adapted beyond all recognition. There's a better way: Focus on the principles, and then develop the practices and tools you need to fulfill them. Otherwise, the teams who adopt practices and tools blindly will end up in trouble when they don't work.

When a Team Is in Trouble, Believe Them

When we ask hardware teams what it was like to use Agile Software Development practices and tools, they describe the challenges of force-fitting work into arbitrary time buckets that don't make sense. They talk about the frustrations of daily standup meetings when things are just not moving that fast because they're waiting on parts, prototype builds or test results.

They describe trying to translate their activities into things like "demos," "user stories" and "work packages," as those concepts get stretched beyond all recognition in order to accommodate their work. This only muddies the waters for everyone. If a "user story" can be anything, the necessary rigor to write a good user story gets lost where it's needed most.

They describe producing demos just to have something to show at a Demo Event, keeping secret GANTT charts to manage dependencies and resource utilization, and backlogs that blow up when they're forced to work at a task level that doesn't make sense in the context of their work. They wonder if they really need to spend so much time managing a backlog that is highly constrained by those dependencies and resources.

Instead of growing more agile — more flexible and responsive — they've become tied down to a method that isn't working for them.

If You Don't Know What Doesn't Fit, You Don't Know Why It Works

If you don't know where a framework or methodology doesn't work, then you don't really know where it *does* work, *why* it works or what problem it actually solves.

We recognize that if you're up to your elbows in UX design for a SaaS app, you don't need Rapid Learning Cycles — you need Agile, because you need short, fast cycles of iteration and immediate feedback. If you're building an airplane that's nearly the same as the last twenty you've built, you need a good GANTT chart. But if you're in Early Development or Advanced Research, working in areas of high uncertainty, then you're right in the sweet spot for Rapid Learning Cycles. (And if you're developing something that cuts across these boundaries, you need a common interface. In Chapter Six, we'll share the Integration Train as a way to bring all the pieces together.)

We know all of this because we know why Agile, GANTT charts, Rapid Learning Cycles and Integration Trains work — which problems they solve and how they solve them. By the end of this book, you will, too.

Agile Practices for Physical Products that Are Proven to Work

The practices we've incorporated into this book have been tested on real physical product development teams. Those teams worked in a variety of industries — from consumer electronics and kitchen appliances to pharma and biotech to solar energy systems, aerospace and medical devices. We have some companies that have been consistently using Rapid Learning Cycles for more than ten years, with measurable reductions in time-to-market of greater than 50 percent over those years. More important, they've rebuilt their confidence in their ability to deliver innovation.

"It didn't just get products out faster," said SunPower's then-PMO Director Celia Cheng in a video interview. "It helped us get the right products out faster."

In 2020, Kairos Power, a next-generation nuclear power startup, wrote our methods directly into an application that led to a $300 million grant from the U.S. Department of Energy to build their first full-scale nuclear prototype, years earlier than expected.

"We have observed that the conventional nuclear development cycle is long, slow and capital-intensive," said then-Engineering Testing Senior Manager Nicolas Zweibaum in a press release. "At Kairos Power, we are disrupting this cycle by adopting a rapid, iterative approach to accelerate design, test and building. Our approach leverages multiple design-build-test cycles with non-nuclear and nuclear systems prior to the first commercial reactor. Since 2019, Kairos has been working with Rapid Learning Cycles to reduce development risk associated with some of its most complex systems."

This book shares the experiments we ran, the successes we had, and also some failures we experienced along the way that helped deepen our understanding of why it's not enough to say *Just. Use. Agile.*

What Problem Are You Solving?

By all means, your software teams should probably be using Agile, especially for anything that benefits from fast, iterative development cycles with rapid feedback. This will help your software teams become more agile — more flexible and responsive. When they do that, they don't just deliver value faster. They deliver the *right* value — the value that will make the most difference to customers and the business — faster.

Your hardware teams, on the other hand, should be using Rapid Learning Cycles to reduce uncertainty in Early Development. When they move into the Execution phases, they can integrate with the software teams, who are using Agile, without force-fitting the wrong tools to their own work.

Finally, we know engineers and scientists are smart people. They won't be confused or overwhelmed by more than one framework for organizing their teams. They'll be relieved by the ability to use the right tool for the job at hand. They're capable of knowing when they're in Agile Software Development space, when they're running Rapid Learning Cycles and when they need a GANTT chart.

This book shares our experiences adapting Agile principles to physical product development so that your teams can realize the promises of agility, becoming more flexible and responsive. When they do that, they don't just get their products to market faster. They get the right products to market faster.

CHAPTER ONE

When Agile Gets Physical

Most of what passes for "Agile for Hardware" is really Scrum for hardware: Organize work into sprints, manage tasks with backlogs, and perform the "ceremonies" of Agile (daily scrums, etc.) In other words, hardware teams are simply asked to conform to a process built for software.

And we get that because in 2012, that's where we started, too. But when it became clear that didn't work, we both asked "why?" We arrived at this common question from two different starting points. Katherine had been active in the Lean Product Development community for some time but was growing dissatisfied with the lack of consistent results and wondered if Agile principles could help. Kathy had just retired from Hewlett-Packard where she'd been part of an innovative team that used Agile principles to improve hardware/software integration.

The answer we discovered was transformative.

Our Starting Point: Scrum

Scrum is the Agile method that Katherine had personally used the most, so when the call came to apply Lean and Agile to an Advanced R&D organization doing basic scientific research, that's what she started with. She pulled in Kathy to leverage her experience applying Agile at the interface of hardware and software for HP's inkjet and laser printer teams. They started with practices and tools that will look familiar to any Agile practitioner:

- Four-week sprints
- Daily standups, which quickly became weekly standups
- Backlog of work packages to be done, which rolled up into larger packages
- Kanban board for tracking progress on tasks within a sprint
- Sprint Demo, Planning Session and Retrospective Events at the end of a sprint

We attempted to use story points to calculate velocity and a burndown chart to track progress, but those practices were quickly abandoned because they didn't generate any useful information. And there were more challenges. At first, we thought these were the normal problems teams have when settling into the process. But it soon became clear that we had bigger issues.

Much of the execution of a work package spent a lot of time in a Waiting state for reasons that were outside the team's control — for supplies, for equipment, for external analysis, for feedback from reviewers, etc. Not all of this waiting time was predictable. So, in practice, the researchers had several things In Progress or Waiting at the same time — and on the kanban board (see Figure 1.1), it didn't look like the team made much progress week-to-week.

Some of the experiments took a long time — much more than a single sprint — with hands-on involvement the entire time. A software team handles this problem by breaking work down into smaller pieces so that all work packages take one sprint or less. For this team, it didn't make sense to break an experiment into smaller pieces. That just made the experiments harder to manage. They were also more expensive to run, in both time and money. Figure 1.2 shows the breakdown of things that could be planned.

Activity

Research Area	Backlog	In Progress	Waiting	Done
Area A				
Area B				
Area C				
Area D				

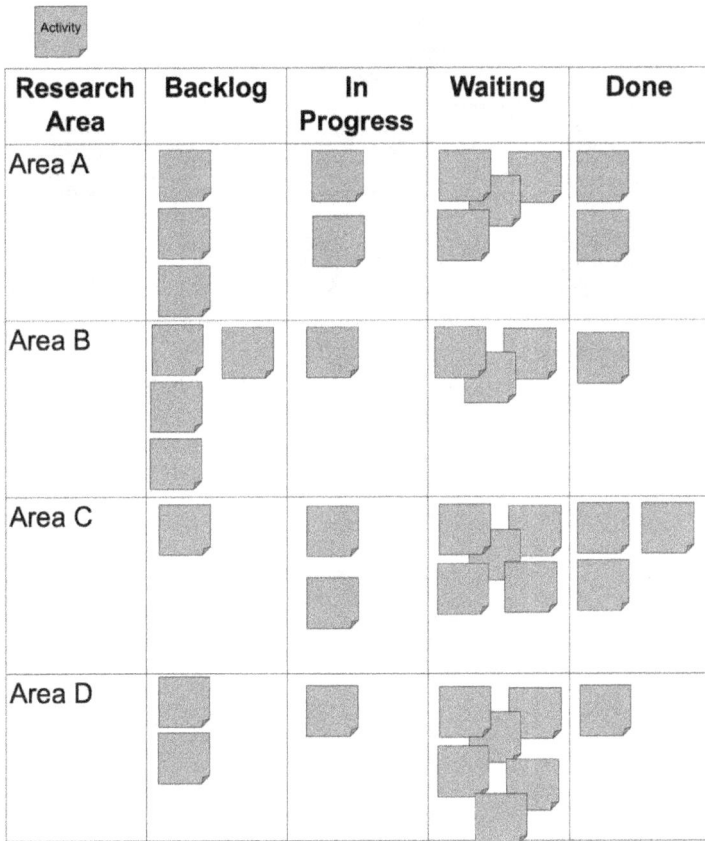

Figure 1.1: Kanban Board at Activity Level with Too Much Waiting

Most experiments were not independent. They were part of complicated dependency chains that constrained the backlog. An Agile backlog doesn't have a good way of tying related items together. We could address simple dependencies through prioritization, but that was clearly inadequate to manage the program. We drew a diagram (Figure 1.3) to visualize the chain of dependencies.

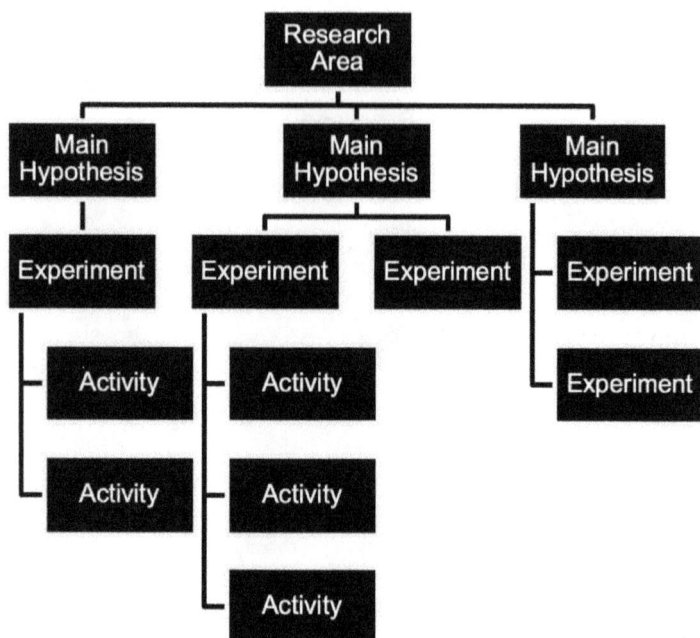

Figure 1.2: What Level to Plan?

The team was an alliance of specialists who could help each other in small ways but could not actually do each other's work. Sprint planning was more an exercise of asking these individuals to make their own sprint plans but without giving them the visibility into dependencies they needed to make good decisions on their own.

Despite these shortcomings, they liked the process. They liked the ceremonies as times to get together, learn about each other's results and get coordinated. The visualization of their work had been a revelation. They, and their managers, could see what they were doing at any point in time, and that was helpful for them.

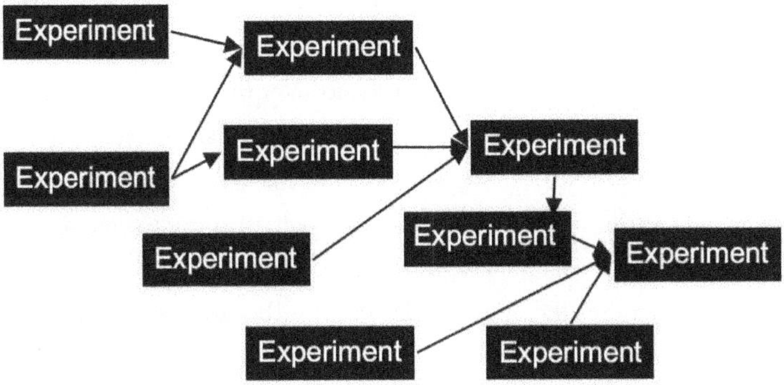

Figure 1.3: Dependency Chain of Experiments

So, this team didn't abandon Scrum. Instead, they began to transform it. Katherine accelerated their progress by running experiments with teams at other companies — also making products that had to be produced in the physical world — then feeding back the results.

Along the way, we had three core breakthroughs that pointed the way towards how to use Agile for physical products:

1. Ask *"What will you learn?"* instead of *"What will you do?"*
2. Make decisions at the right time, with the right people and the best available knowledge.
3. Visualize the flow of knowledge from idea to launch.

The First Breakthrough: "What Will You Learn?"

We were fortunate to work with an Advanced R&D lab first because the entire mission of such an entity is to learn and then share what's learned. All the burden of execution belongs to others. This made the lab a clean test case for how to apply Agile principles to an organization that generates value by building knowledge.

Software teams also generate value by creating knowledge in the form of things like algorithms and user interface designs. But they have a natural repository for that knowledge in the form of their code library. Once that library has been developed, it can be replicated and reused over and over, with little or no expense. They can test the library using automated regression testing, and they can easily change it, then test to determine if the change had any unintended side effects.

That's not the kind of knowledge the lab's Research team built. They were working to build knowledge around a biological process, in vitro, so that their company could perhaps identify a target for drug therapy. They were running biochemical experiments that attempted to model human biology, but these lab experiments were well understood to be models. There would be years of work to turn this knowledge into a new therapy, and the final result would look nothing like the models. But without this foundational work to answer important questions about these biological processes, those therapies could never be developed.

What Are the Critical Questions?

This Research team had a portfolio that called out specific sets of questions to answer. The scientists on the team designed experiments to answer these questions, technicians carried out the lab work and data collection and the scientists analyzed the results.

These stages lent themselves to a kanban board using columns for Backlog, Experimental Design, Experiment, Analysis and Done (Figure 1.4).

So far, so good. But these experiments were expensive and time-consuming, with the risk that an experiment would lead to inconclusive results. The team reduced that risk via peer reviews and some external reviews before the experiments were run, but even Experimental Design took several weeks. The experiments themselves took much longer. The team quickly realized that the kanban board wasn't helping as much as they thought. They could see the work on the board, and at first that had been exciting. But the work wasn't moving.

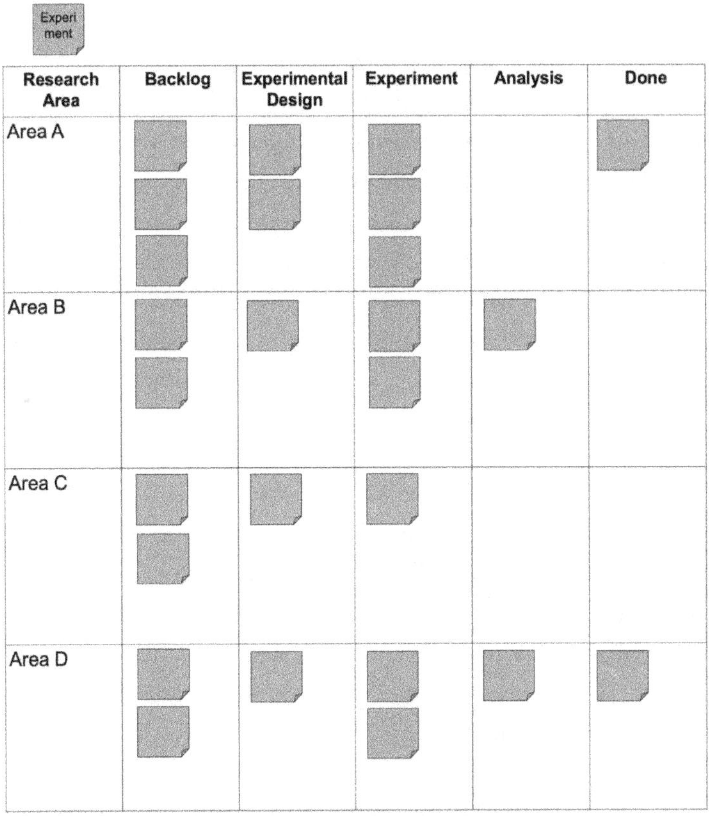

Experi ment					

Research Area	Backlog	Experimental Design	Experiment	Analysis	Done
Area A	▢ ▢ ▢	▢ ▢	▢ ▢ ▢		▢
Area B	▢ ▢	▢	▢ ▢	▢	
Area C	▢ ▢	▢	▢		
Area D	▢ ▢	▢	▢ ▢	▢	▢

Figure 1.4: Kanban Board with Experiments

Visualize the Flow of Questions to Optimize the Flow of Knowledge
One solution that's often used in situations like this is to break down the work packages into smaller pieces that move more often. The team didn't like that idea. Viewing individual tasks wasn't helpful, and optimizing the flow of specific tasks wasn't the best way to speed up their research. Instead, they fine-tuned their process in two ways.

The first involved the sequence of the questions themselves. The answers to one question fed into other questions. Visualizing this sequence made it much more obvious where they had opportunities to optimize the sequence of their experiments. The sequence changed often, so sticky notes on a whiteboard was the best way to manage this flow. They quickly ditched the backlog, replacing it with a simple sticky note diagram showing how the experiments flowed into each other (Figure 1.5).

The second way to speed up involved the Experimental Design, when the experiments were planned. That presented an opportunity to consider a different approach, such as a smaller, rougher experiment to validate an idea before doing a more extensive, rigorous experiment.

The two shifts transformed the focus of a sprint from doing to learning. Instead of "How much can we get done?" the team started asking "How much can we learn?"

"How Much Can We Learn?" Changes the Game

Teams stopped focusing so much on specific activities inside work packages. Instead, they began challenging themselves to learn more, and more deeply. They began challenging each other: "Do we need this long experiment, or can we run this shorter experiment first? Maybe if we learn enough, we don't need the long experiment." They began finding faster, cheaper ways to learn. They started to become a lot more effective, as measured by their research productivity.

On the Lean side, Dr. Allen Ward had long advocated for the practice of building knowledge prior to making decisions on a development program. His research at Toyota showed that company teams there spent much less time in rework loops of revisited decisions. Instead of making decisions early and waiting to the end to validate their decisions, they tried to learn as much as they could before committing to a decision. As a result, Toyota was able to speed through execution of a new car model with far fewer problems in late development than their peers.

Most product development has a lot of long learning cycles. Teams make decisions in Early Development that don't get validated until later in the process. Then they have to go backwards to fix the problem, causing project delays, cost overruns and disappointing results.

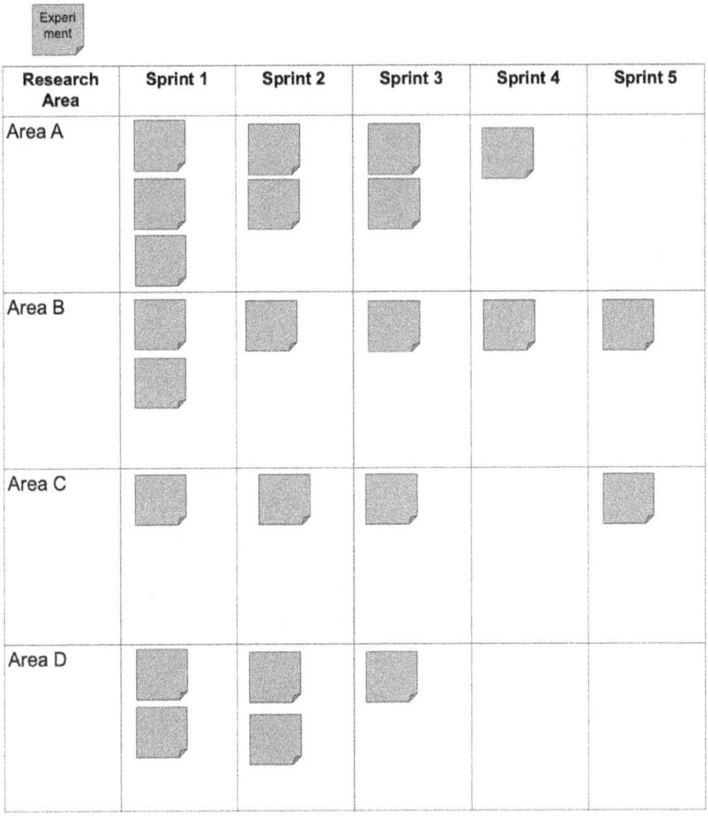

Research Area	Sprint 1	Sprint 2	Sprint 3	Sprint 4	Sprint 5
Area A	▪▪▪	▪▪	▪▪	▪	
Area B	▪▪	▪	▪	▪	▪
Area C	▪	▪	▪		▪
Area D	▪▪	▪▪	▪		

Figure 1.5: Time-Based Flow of Experiments

This problem is inherent to waterfall development in both hardware and software. It is, in fact, the very problem that the early proponents of Agile Software Development wanted to eliminate, and the reason why waterfall is a dirty word in the Agile world. The solution to this problem in both hardware and software is the same — shorten the time from decision to validation — but the implementation for hardware is completely different.

Build Knowledge Before Making Decisions to Eliminate Waterfall Development

The inherent problem of waterfall development is that it forces a team to make decisions without the knowledge needed to make those decisions with confidence. The solution is to wait to finalize decisions until you have the knowledge you need. Katherine first encountered the concept of the Last Responsible Moment in the writings of Mary Poppendieck. Her books on Lean Software Development use Lean principles (with references to Dr. Ward's research) to explain why Agile works.

Agile software teams solve the problems with waterfall by building their software incrementally, making only the decisions around the specific work packages they've chosen to complete in a sprint. They delay even the decisions about which work packages or user stories to implement, choosing them out of a backlog at the start of each sprint. They get immediate feedback, first from their own tests and then from the users at a Demo to validate their decisions. When the code passes all the tests, and users have validated that it works for them, then it's done-done.

The lab's Research team started out with a similar approach but soon realized that the knowledge they were building could not be validated in a single cycle. Individual work tasks could be done-done, but that wouldn't improve the quality of their decisions or help them optimize the flow of knowledge through their research program. The answers to the question "What did you do yesterday?" were not very interesting or useful to a team that is so focused on building knowledge.

Instead, we worked together to design a system that delivered better answers to the question "What are we learning?" so that the team could make better decisions about the direction of their research. The first breakthrough element of the Rapid Learning Cycles system was in place.

The Second Breakthrough: "Right Time, Right People, Best Available Knowledge"

The Research team's work was going well, but when Katherine applied the lessons from "Scrum for Knowledge Work" to a product development team's work — with hard deadlines and deliverables — this learning-driven approach proved to be necessary but insufficient. The structure made it possible to implement Dr. Ward's vision for "learning before commitment," but teams were overwhelmed by the number of questions they had to answer before they could commit.

They had little in the way of knowledge that they could reuse since most of it was locked inside the brains of the more experienced engineers or in inaccessible systems. Even if they did intend to reuse a technical solution, there wasn't much available to explain how it worked or why the original team had made their design decisions. So, they essentially needed to learn everything.

The first boards had too many questions in the backlog, and then once they made it from the backlog into a sprint, the questions took a long time to close. This led to a "snowplow" effect in which the numbers of unclosed questions grew and grew until the system collapsed. Katherine could facilitate a team through this only by helping them ruthlessly prioritize, but how did they know which questions were the most important ones to answer?

The Right Questions to Answer

As we experimented with different ways to filter the questions, Katherine saw that the potential impact of a question on a program's direction was an obvious selection criterion. But how could we know whether a given question had high impact or low impact, especially if it wasn't obvious? After looking at one complex program in particular that had nearly snowplowed its way past a major milestone, Katherine noticed that the questions that made the most difference were the ones that would drive an important decision.

On a typical program, these decisions would be made, usually a lot earlier, without the knowledge the team was trying to build. But it would be a decision on shaky ground, one that a good program manager would treat as a risky decision. If it was a major decision, it would have to be revisited if the risk of a wrong decision materialized. And if that decision had too many unanswered questions around it — leaving the original decision on very shaky ground — it probably would be revisited later, when more information came in.

Yet it was treated all along like a final decision, so every revisited decision was treated like an exception to the normal process, which created a lot of disruption. Good Project Leaders added buffers and margins to deal with the inevitable problems, but all too often the buffers and margins would get eliminated in a misguided attempt to go faster or consumed by the first few decisions that needed to be changed.

The Impact of Revisiting a Final Decision Is Much Higher in Hardware

When a major decision needs to be changed late in development on a physical product, that change comes with a lot of cost. The decision has been embedded into the product, with other decisions made that depend on it. Change is usually neither quick nor simple. It may require doing something that significantly delays the program or increases the per-unit cost. The team may have to cut a desirable feature or compromise on the user experience in order to get the product out at all — much less on time.

We've come to think of decisions like that as long, slow learning cycles. As Figure 1.6 shows, we make decisions early in development that don't get validated until much later in development. When we find out that we have to revisit the decision, we sometimes have to loop back to much earlier stages of development to fix the problem, adjusting the requirements, specs, or product design.

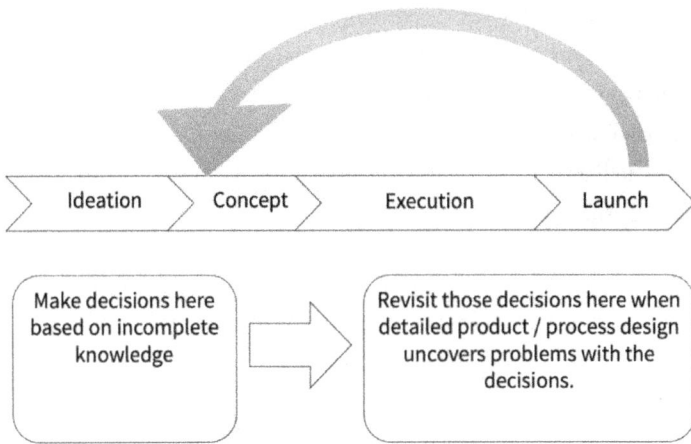

Figure 1.6: Long, Slow Loopbacks

Teams sometimes try to fix these execution challenges by changing the execution process in some way or, even worse, by locking down requirements to avoid late design changes. But these fixes don't work because the problem is not rooted in the execution process, and normally it's not an option to just ignore the needed change — at least if the team wants to release a viable product.

The only way to eliminate the problem is to eliminate these long, slow loopbacks at their source: decisions made without the knowledge needed to make the decisions with confidence. When teams can do that, they run into far fewer obstacles during the Execution phases.

They don't even have to get it perfect — they just have to eliminate enough of these late-found defects to avoid overwhelming the team's capacity to make changes. One of these is not usually enough to drive a product development program over the edge, but a handful —especially if they're all interconnected — can trigger enough design instability to tip the product over into an endless series of "build-test-fix" cycles with no end in sight.

The way to eliminate these long, slow loopbacks is to make these major decisions at the right time with the best available knowledge. We started calling these Key Decisions — decisions that teams need to make with confidence to avoid long, slow loopbacks. The Key Decision Matrix shown in Figure 1.7 helps teams identify the high-impact, high-unknown Key Decisions that could trigger long, slow loopbacks.

High Impact
on the Business Case

Known
Solutions

Key
Decisions

High
Known

High
Unknown

"No
Brainer"
Decisions

Best
Guess
Decisions

Low Impact
on the Business Case

Figure 1.7: Key Decision Matrix

The concept of a Key Decision went a long way towards eliminating the "snowplow" effect of too many questions that made too little difference to the program. The team was not overwhelmed with too many unanswered yet unimportant questions to close. Instead, they focused on the questions they needed to answer to make Key Decisions with confidence.

Decisions at the Right Time with the Right People

When we added a directive to make these Key Decisions at the right time, we found we could delay many of them, and that they were even less likely to be revisited if they were made as late as possible. Finally, we began asking teams to be more conscious about who needed to make a Key Decision and especially which stakeholders needed to be engaged for a decision to be a good one.

When the first teams began making Key Decisions at the right time, with the right people and the best available knowledge, we started seeing performance improve. Teams hit their milestones on time and ultimately released the product faster. They spent less time churning in late development on revisited decisions. They were able to make better decisions about cost, features and performance, which meant the products did better in the market. And they were able to do all of this without any additional resources — the development budgets and teams were the same.

Much Better — and Much More Potential

The teams were happy because they were getting better results, but Katherine could see that the process still wasn't working as well as it could. Teams were still spending too long in the learning phases and arriving at major decision points without the knowledge they needed.

The Third Breakthrough: Multilevel, Time-Based Planning

Up to this point, we had assumed that all these questions and decisions would go into a backlog that the team would manage in the same way that software teams manage their backlog of user stories. As soon as we had the right questions to answer, we could see that wasn't enough. We also needed to visualize *when* each question needed to be answered so that we could make decisions at the right time.

Agile methods, including Scrum, usually employ a backlog: a prioritized list of work packages or user stories. In the software world, the best work packages and user stories are independent of each other: They can be executed in any order. And on a Software Development team, the person assigned to implement a user story is, to some extent, flexible. You may have people who are stronger in one area than another, but, for the most part, they can all write tests, write code and offer intelligent feedback when reviewing others' code.

Agile Software Development Assumes Independent Work

In pure Scrum, the user stories represent independent features that can be implemented in any order — so the correct order is the one that will deliver the most customer value earliest in the program. The Product Owner takes on the role of determining what customer value will be delivered in a sprint (the Sprint Goal), and the team pulls the user stories out of the backlog that they need to deliver this value (the Sprint Plan).

This works well to the extent that the user stories are truly independent, and the team members are truly flexible to deliver any user story. In practice, Agile teams work to improve the independence of their user stories as one way to improve the effectiveness of Agile itself.

It's rarely this clean, even in software. Some things (security, basic architecture work) have to be done first. And you don't want to keep a user interface designer idle because the Sprint Plan calls for improving key algorithms to deliver faster, more accurate results. So, most teams do allow the User Interface Designer to work ahead on some things while the others work on the guts of the algorithms. But most of the time, resources are flexible enough and the dependencies are simple enough to manage this in a backlog.

Physical Product Developers Have Dependencies to Manage

Physical product development has many more dependencies and much more inflexibility. We've seen over and over again that physical product developers end up tripping over the backlog for this very reason. The backlog can only manage the simplest of dependencies via prioritization: I must do A before B; therefore A has a higher priority than B until A is done. What happens if B is also dependent on C, which is dependent on both A and D, and so on? If you don't visualize this network of dependencies, it's hard to even recognize most of them.

In some of the worst cases, the teams have completely lost track of their dependencies, to the point of failing to deliver the CAD models needed to build major system prototypes in time to start production. More often, we've seen that the Project Leader has a GANTT chart hidden away someplace where their misguided Agile Coach can't find it. This hidden GANTT chart drives the Sprint Plan even though the team is performing all the "ceremonies" of backlog-based planning.

Why Do We Need a Backlog When We Have a Plan?

In 2011, Katherine interviewed Philips' Suzanne van Egmond for her first book, *The Mastery of Innovation*. Van Egmond had developed a system called "Lean Scheduling" that combined the best of backlog-based planning with the need for a schedule. The distinguishing feature was a multilevel plan:

- Level 0 Plan that covered the entire program through launch and production ramp, which forecast the team's path through the Philips phase-gate process
- Level 1 Plan that covered the current phase of work, typically six months or so in Early Development, focused on the decisions that needed to be made in this current phase to hit the next gate
- Level 2 Plan that focused on the major activities and deliverables for the next quarter or so within this plan
- Level 3 Plan that represented the activities to be done on a daily basis for the next sprint, which could be managed on a kanban board

PHILIPS

Lean Scheduling

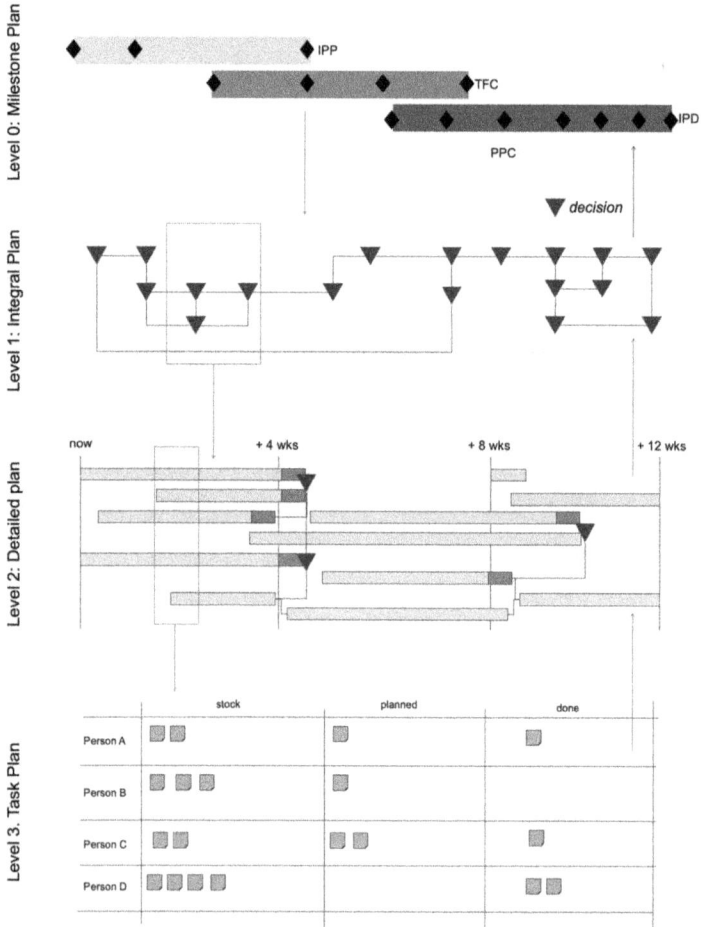

From *Mastery of Innovation*, p. 111. Used by Permission.

Figure 1.8: Multilevel Plan from the Philips Case Study in
The Mastery Of Innovation

There was no backlog, except at Level 3, and that backlog was populated from the work to be done in the Level 2 plan. Everything else was mapped out on a rolling basis: the Level 1 Plan when the team entered a new phase, the Level 2 plan once a quarter, the Level 3 plan once a sprint.

Could Lean Scheduling transform an Agile plan into something that worked for physical products?

Some Agile Software Development methods also use multilevel plans but for a different purpose. They are managing a continuous stream of value delivery over a period of months or years. The top-level plans map out customer releases, and the lower-level plans map out the work required to deliver those releases. These plans are grounded in the assumption that an individual work package or user story, defined at the lowest level, can be completed within a sprint. The work packages roll up into epics, which roll up into Program Increments in methods like SAFe® and ultimately into customer releases.

None of this is true for physical product development. The purpose of the multilevel plan is to map out the entire path a single product will take from idea through Feasibility, Product Design, Process Design, Production and Launch.

Physical Product Development Plans Map Out the Path to Launch
With the addition of a project plan that mapped out the path to launch without over-constraining it, we had a stable structure that began to deliver repeatable results. This third breakthrough gave the teams the visibility they needed to maximize the value of the time they had to learn. When we introduced it to physical product development teams, they either got faster or they knew exactly what had gotten in the way. They had far fewer long, slow loopbacks, and when they did encounter one, they could trace it back to its root cause to keep it from happening on future programs.

They were able to achieve this because they knew what decisions they needed to make, when they needed to make those decisions, and what knowledge they needed to make the best possible decisions. Then they had an actionable plan to build that knowledge, a structure to ensure the knowledge got built, and the right events for sharing knowledge and making decisions.

And we knew why all of this worked to increase agility — flexibility and responsiveness — for hardware teams: It was grounded in the principles of Agile that deliver fast, flexible flow.

CHAPTER TWO

Fast, Flexible Flow

We both have scientific backgrounds, and we both know that it's not enough for an experiment to deliver the results we want. We also have to understand the mechanism — the reason why the experiment gives us these results. When we understand *why*, it's easier to understand *how* to leverage this knowledge for new situations, where the same conditions don't apply.

When Kathy first started using Agile Software Development methods on small single-team projects, the method worked well, as described in the Agile books of that time. When she got involved in larger multi-team Agile projects, she saw new problems — and the why in the books of the time didn't provide workable solutions. Without a good why, the teams kept trying different fixes that didn't work well.

Then one day her new manager handed her Don Reinertsen's book, *Managing the Design Factory*, and after some reading, she realized that the mechanism behind many of the practices in Agile Software Development could be explained by queueing theory. Once she understood the mechanism, queueing theory suggested different solutions. When the teams tried those solutions, they worked — and her fellow team members understood why.

Queueing theory explains how batches of work flow through a system. The principles underneath queueing theory have been demonstrated to work in a variety of areas, from telecommunications to highway traffic flow to project management. In each area, the principles apply, but the specific practices and tools are specific to the context of application, which has its own set of assumptions. Agile Software Development embodies the principles of queueing theory in its methods, practices and tools.

Why Do Agile Methods Work in Software?

The first thing Kathy observed was that Agile Software Development methods organize development work into small batches, then seek to optimize the flow of the batches through the development process. That's exactly what queueing theory recommends. Agile used the principles of queueing theory to solve the specific problems that software teams have within the context of a software development program. Once Kathy recognized this, her work on printers at HP gave her opportunities to explore these ideas in more depth.

A "batch" is just a collection of work that's produced all at the same time. Most people are familiar with batches of cookies. A batch of cookies is a set of ingredients that a baker gathers, mixes, shapes and bakes at the same time, going from unmixed ingredients to raw cookie dough to cookies altogether. Most bakers learn as children that it's not this neat: A full batch of cookies can't fit onto a cookie sheet, so the large batch of dough in the mixing bowl gets broken up into oven-sized batches of baking cookies.

In the days before Agile, software development teams worked on large batches of features and functionality that would take months or years. They would try to gather and write up all the requirements, then create a complete architectural design. Only then would they start coding. At the end, they'd bring all the pieces of code together into an integrated system. Finally, they'd test the entire system — and find a lot of problems.

The team would have to try to find the source of each problem in the midst of this complex integrated system. They might have to loop back to coding or to the architecture. Often, they'd have to loop back all the way to requirements because the users couldn't explain what they needed. Users are notoriously incapable of fully defining the requirements for a system they haven't seen yet.

When teams work like this, it's like asking bakery staff to buy ingredients and mix an entire year's worth of cookie dough at one time before they start to bake any cookies. By the time they put the cookies into the oven, the ingredients are no longer fresh. And customers may now want a different type of cookie.

In fact, it's worse than that because a good baker will at least taste the dough to make sure it's good before putting any cookies into the oven. A team that's following a strict waterfall process may not do any system integration or system-level testing before most of the design and coding work is done.

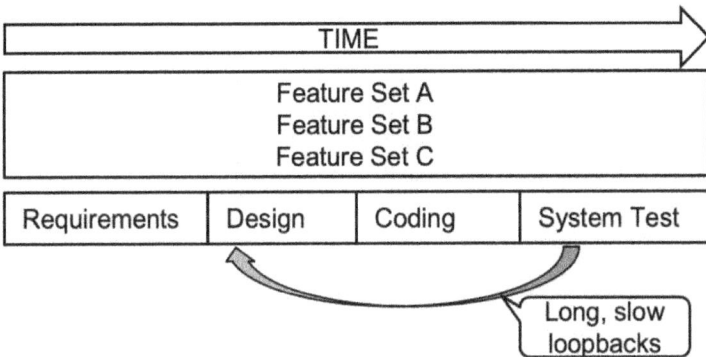

Figure 2.1: Waterfall Development Works in One Large Batch with Long, Slow Loopbacks

Agile Software Development Splits Work into Small, Independent Batches

Agile methods split the product into small batches of features and functionality, often structured as "user stories." They work on just a few small batches at a time and drive those batches to completion before starting the next batches. This small set of features go all the way through requirements, design, coding, integration and system testing in just a few hours to a few weeks. When something goes wrong, the loopback is a few weeks at most instead of months or even years.

Teams can find causes for these problems faster because they haven't built very much. The design and the code are still fresh. The errors haven't propagated across dozens of inter-related features. This makes it much easier to fix the problems. Because the team doesn't get stuck at the end with a bunch of problems that are now complex and difficult to diagnose, they are able to deliver the product a lot faster. The shorter loopbacks speed up development and improve quality at the same time.

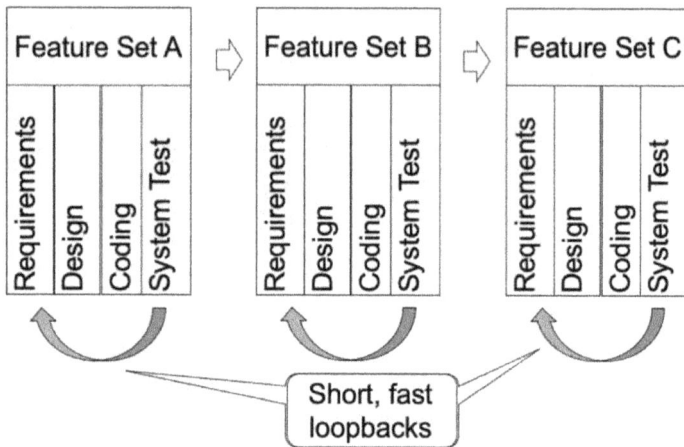

Figure 2.2: Agile Software Development Works in Small Batches with Short, Fast Loopbacks

Agile achieves speed, flexibility and responsiveness by working in small batches — just as predicted by queueing theory. The batches are small and independent with few dependencies between them. A team invests very little time and effort in a batch before it goes into development. Prior to that, the batch exists as just a short description with some acceptance criteria. The team has not spent much time at all gathering detailed requirements or doing design work. Instead, they wait to do this work until it's needed to start a batch.

Bakers know that they make the best cookies with fresh ingredients that go quickly from the mixing bowl into the oven. They'll have happier customers and more profitable bakeries if they are responsive to changing customer needs. Software developers also have happier customers when they gather requirements and then get user feedback on the implementation while the requirements are still fresh.

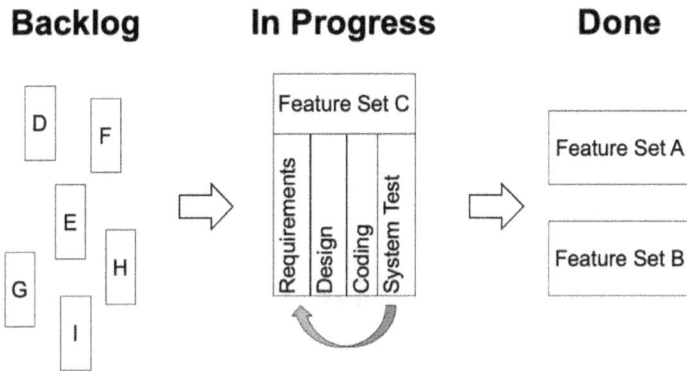

Figure 2.3: Working in Small Batches Allows the Plan to Be Easily Changed

As the team learns more about their customers, and business needs change, they have the option to drop any features that customers don't really need without losing much investment or affecting work already done. They can substitute features that customers need more without too much trouble. The team can rearrange the order of the batches whenever it makes sense.

If you've ever been an early adopter of a new app or web service, you may have seen this in action. Chances are the first version of the product — the minimum viable product (MVP) — didn't do very much. But every update of the app layered in new features, as the team fixed defects from previous releases. Meanwhile, they gathered feedback from you and other early users to figure out which features they should add, which improvements they should make to the user interface, and which defects were most important to fix first.

They're able to do this because their batches are largely independent of each other — there are few dependencies within feature sets. Small batches create speed, flexibility and responsiveness for software projects. Most of the other practices and tools within Agile build on this foundation of small, *relatively independent* batches.

The fundamental batch of a software project is often called a "user story." User stories describe one single feature from a user's perspective. Software developers write user stories in a specific way that's known to optimize the process of developing that feature. There are entire books written about how to write good user stories.

In software, the behavior of the entire organization can be described in terms of user stories. As Figure 2.4 shows, there is essentially only one major workstream. That workstream produces completed user stories, which quickly translate into revenue. They don't have to worry about manufacturing, distribution or warranty returns. Their workstreams to release, install and support a product are much simpler than they are for a physical product.

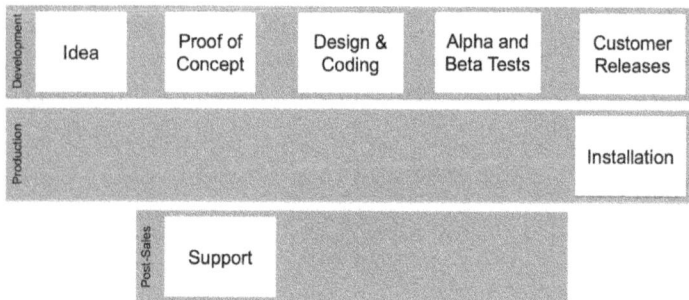

Development	Idea	Proof of Concept	Design & Coding	Alpha and Beta Tests	Customer Releases
Production					Installation
Post-Sales		Support			

Figure 2.4: In a Software Product, Nearly Everything Happens Within a Single Workstream

And this is also where the assumptions of Agile don't hold true for physical product development: It's much more difficult to develop a physical product by breaking it down into a single workstream of relatively independent features.

Hardware Projects Don't Have a Single Type of Batch

Imagine trying to develop and deliver the braking function of a golf cart without the rest of the golf cart. How could you be sure that it works? How could you be sure that it will continue to work as reliably as it needs to work, even after accounting for natural variation in the production and assembly processes?

For a modern golf cart, a braking system requires input from mechanical, electrical, firmware and manufacturing engineers who are all doing different but highly interdependent work in parallel. No matter how good their CAD tools are, eventually they must build and test the product in the physical world. They need a manufacturing process to assemble the system over and over. They need a supply chain to procure the materials and components.

Then that system, now part of a full golf cart, will be physically shipped to the customer — with intermediate stops at distributors and resellers along the way. When it's time to replace the brake pads, the replacements also have to be sourced and shipped to service centers staffed with technicians who can install the pads. Those technicians will go to the golf courses to install the pads on the carts.

Figure 2.5 shows how many more types of things need to be done to design, deliver and support a physical product. These things require different engineering disciplines. Such a complicated system doesn't have a single type of batch flowing through a single workstream.

Development	Idea	Proof of Concept	Detailed Design	Lab Prototypes	Production Prototypes
Production	Sourcing	Mass Production	Finished Goods Inventory	Distribution and Channels	Customer's Physical Location
Post-Sales		Support	Warranty and Service	End of Life Disposal	

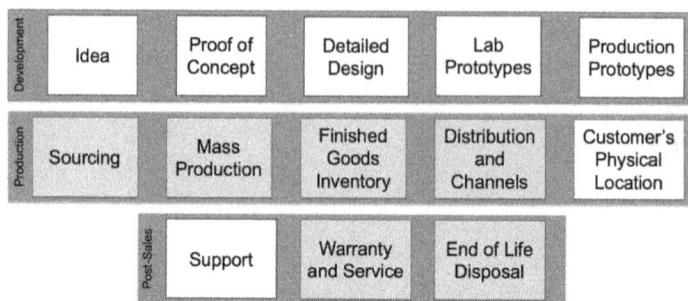

Figure 2.5: Physical Products Have More Complex Lifecycles that Involve More Disciplines

Where Are the Batches and Workflows for Physical Products?

If hardware teams want to become faster, more flexible and more responsive, they need a different way of thinking about batches and workflows. Queueing theory can help us see more useful ways of splitting work into smaller batches inside workflows that will give us those short, fast loops that drive flexibility and responsiveness. They won't look like the user stories of a software development team, but they are grounded in the same principles.

To get started, it's helpful to know a little about where queueing theory came from and how it's been embedded into Agile Software Development. It all started with telephone circuits.

A Quick History of Queueing Theory

In the early 1900s, Agner Krarup Erlang, a Danish mathematician and engineer, realized that if he thought of telephone calls as small, independent batches of work, he could apply statistical methods to optimize the flow of calls through circuits and operators.

In Erlang's time, telephone operators and circuits were scarce resources, so calls queued up as they waited for a free operator and a free line. Erlang realized that he could use statistical methods to understand how calls flowed through a given system, then use this understanding to predict how the system would respond to changes.

Erlang built mathematical models of the telephone systems and then changed different parameters to see what happened. This allowed him to predict what would happen when the telephone company changed the flow, by adding more operators or circuits, increasing an operator's capacity or by changing the way that calls were assigned to resources.

These mathematical models became the foundations of queueing theory. They study what happens to batches of work that flow through a system, especially when a batch has to wait for a resource to become available. When there aren't enough resources to immediately process all the incoming batches, the unprocessed batches have to wait in line for their turn — or as they say in the UK, they "queue up."

A bowl of unbaked cookie dough contains a "queue" of unbaked cookies waiting for space on a cookie sheet to go into the oven. A traffic jam contains a visible queue of cars waiting to pass through a bottleneck, like the single open lane after a collision.

Queueing theory revolutionized telecommunications. Many decades after Erlang built his first models, people in other fields began to realize that their systems displayed behavior that could also be predicted by queueing theory. It's been used to optimize the flow of travelers in an airport and the flow of cars through freeway systems. Lean manufacturing applies these principles to production environments. Agile Software Development applies this theory to the process of building software systems. They all share the common understanding that systems deliver value by completing batches of work. In some fields, the initial pioneers started working smaller batches before they realized that queueing theory recommended exactly the same steps — and could go further.

Value, Value, Value

To optimize any system using queueing theory, you must do one critical thing: Define your batches so that each batch delivers value *on its own*.

A "batch" can be lots of different things: the cookies on a cookie sheet, the individual cars stuck in traffic, shopping carts waiting for a free checkout clerk, packets of data flowing through the internet. These are all things someone actually wants: the baked cookie, the on-time arrival at the office, the purchased groceries ready to take home, the download of a loved one's photograph. The system is the means of delivering that value: the baking process, the freeway, the checkout process, the internet.

Queues form wherever a batch can't be processed through the next step because there isn't enough capacity. Queues can form at the start of a process (cookie ingredients waiting to be mixed) or in the middle, when they're partially complete (the car stuck on the freeway on-ramp).

We've already shown that user stories are the most useful batches of work in software. They are small bits of valued functionality that can be created, tested and finished in a short period of time — usually two weeks or less. The small size ensures fast, short feedback loops. A user story is finished when it does what it says it will do, and it is ready to be released to external users. When it's released, it immediately delivers value. This is what happens in many apps when they get updated.

Knowledge Is a Form of Value

But customer value — the value our users get immediately — is only one measure of value. Completed user stories also deliver value from the knowledge created by the user story's implementation. Knowledge creates value when it enables the organization to work more effectively or produce a more valuable product.

In software, the user's response to the finished user stories provides valuable feedback: Does the product do what it's supposed to do? Is it easy to use? Do users now realize that they need something different? Teams also learn how many user stories of a given complexity they can finish in a given week. This helps them predict the end date for the project. That's valuable knowledge for the team's leadership.

In the last chapter, we described how knowledge was the primary value being delivered by the Advanced Research team, and how powerful it was for them to focus on delivering that value in small clearly defined batches. To understand why that was so powerful, it's helpful to first know a little more about the tools of queueing theory.

The Tools of Queueing Theory

Once the work has been split into small batches that deliver value, queueing theory has tools to help get more batches through the system faster with the same resources in the same amount of time. This is called "maximizing the throughput" of the system.

When we realized that the right batches for that Advanced Research team would center around the knowledge being created, it opened the door for us to use these tools to optimize the flow of knowledge creation:

- Optimize batch sizes
- Limit work-in-process
- Put repeating events on a cadence
- Prioritize batches

These tools work together to reduce or eliminate queues and optimize the flow of work through the system. They make the entire process faster, more flexible and more responsive.

Optimize Batch Size

Figure 2.2 showed that smaller batches deliver value sooner — to a point. The output of the batch is available to be used sooner, any new knowledge from that batch is also available sooner to benefit the organization earlier, and less time is spent on loopbacks. In general, small batches are better than large ones, although it is possible to make batch sizes too small. The math behind queueing theory can determine ideal batch sizes, but we don't need that detail for our purposes. It's enough to know that smaller batches are generally better.

For our cookie baking team, small batches reduce the waste generated if the eggs turn out to be spoiled, the oven temperature is too hot or the bake time is too long — but it would take a lot more time and energy to bake only one cookie at a time. The cumulative overhead for each sheet with a single cookie is much higher than the value of the quick feedback. The ideal batch size is more likely to be one or two batches of cookies, sized to fit on a cookie sheet.

For the Advanced Research team in Chapter One, the right batch size turned out to be the Hypothesis-in-Process — an idea they wanted to test. This later developed into the Knowledge Gap, as we will see in Chapter Three.

Limit Your Work-in-Process

The number of batches being worked on at the same time is known as the work-in-process (WIP). If you have too many partially completed things in the system at once, it slows everything down. You've experienced this yourself if you've ever been stuck in slow-moving traffic: There are just too many cars for the road to handle.

When people have too many things to work on, they lose precious time switching from one thing to another. They pay a task-switching hit in productivity every time they have to set aside one thing to reload their brains with the relevant details from the next thing. When too many meetings chop up their available time into small pieces, this can waste an amazing amount of time over a week, leading to the feeling that it's impossible to get anything done except at night or on the weekends.

It may seem like it's faster to start a new batch the instant a resource inside the system has capacity. In practice, this just slows down the entire system. WIP limits work like gates that keep out new batches until the entire system has enough capacity to handle the new batch without slowing down anywhere. The queues build up outside the system, where they are easier to manage and don't trigger task-switching. The resources inside the system work on only the batches already in process until those batches are done.

For our Advanced Development team, this means the number of Hypotheses or Knowledge Gaps in process has to be balanced with the team's capacity to focus and drive these batches to completion.

In practice, this is a little more complicated, even in simple systems like our cookie baking process. Our cookie baking team can minimize WIP by making only the amount of dough that can be baked in the oven at one time, but that generates too much overhead from the need to take out, measure and mix ingredients. It might be better to put the mixing step on a regular cadence.

Put Repeating Events on a Cadence

A cadence is a regular, predictable rhythm within a process. The team's meeting is held every Monday at 10 a.m. The website gets refreshed every fourth Tuesday. Regular, predictable rhythms reduce overhead. They coordinate the work of different parts of the system so that they can work better together. They create a sense of urgency around getting work done that pulls work through a system. They reduce system variability in ways that can help reduce or eliminate queues.

According to queueing theory, cadences primarily work by pulling sets of batches into the system at regular intervals. The rest of the system can then be tuned to that interval to minimize overhead. Everything that needs a customer demonstration will get one at the next Demo, scheduled every other Tuesday at 3 p.m. Everything ready for release will be released every fourth Friday at the end of the day.

This is how on-ramp signals work: They cause cars to enter the freeway on regular, predictable intervals. The regular intervals delay the formation of traffic jams during rush hour and shorten the time it takes for them to resolve. This is why Scrum and other Agile methods use sprints — to establish regular cadences for pulling in user stories.

The natural cadence for our cookie baking team is the time it takes to bake a batch of cookies. The cookie baking process will flow well to the extent that the other steps of the process use the same cadence, even if this means that they are not always doing something. There is no point in filling up more than one extra set of cookie sheets with unbaked cookies if there is no oven space to bake them in.

Our cookie baking team can decide to make enough dough to fill four cookie sheets, trading off the small risk that there could be something wrong at the mixing step for the optimization of fewer times through the mixing steps. The batch size is four filled cookie sheets, and the mixing cadence is then the amount of time it takes to bake a filled cookie sheet times four.

Queueing theory provides tools to calculate the ideal cadence of the system. However, we don't need the math for a typical development program. Instead, we've observed that teams work best with the shortest cadence that doesn't trigger excessive overhead. Software teams started with four-week sprints, but advances in testing automation and other tools have shortened this; some teams are able to release as often as every three days without excessive overhead. Hardware teams usually need longer cadences of two to four weeks, which is where our Advanced Research team ended up.

Prioritize Your Batches

Good WIP limits move queues outside the system, where it's easier to see them and easier to prioritize them. Queuing theory has some specific tools to help with prioritization. The right tools to use depends on the characteristics and interdependencies of our batches. Before we can look at those, we need to find the batches in physical product development.

Where Are the Batches in Physical Product Development?

As we saw in Figure 2.5, there's no reason to think that all the work of creating physical products could be adequately described by a single batch moving through a single workflow. We already have good methods for managing some of these workstreams using batches. In the production workstream, Lean Manufacturing methods draw directly from queueing theory to optimize the flow of work through production processes where the batch is primarily an individual part or a subassembly. Firmware teams (teams writing embedded software) often use Agile methods to optimize their workflow, with user stories as the batch.

You could, and some people such as Don Reinertsen have attempted to, map out the queues inside a development workstream the way you would inside a production workstream. But this only works for production processes because they already have easily recognizable elements that deliver value independently (parts, subassemblies, finished goods, cookies) that can be grouped into batches relatively easily (production runs, cookies on cookie sheets). A manufacturing plant can have many complex workflows, but because you can see the batches, it's easier to spot opportunities to optimize those flows.

Knowledge work doesn't lend itself to neat batches of things that we can easily recognize. The work is far too variable, and the batches are much harder to see. Instead, we look for batches by looking for areas where we observe two conditions:

1. Long, slow loopbacks where late-found problems trigger lots of rework.
2. Large batches of work that could be split into smaller batches that deliver value independently.

This was, in fact, the core insight behind the development of the Rapid Learning Cycles framework: we could eliminate a lot of the churn, project delays, cost overruns and disappointments in late development when we divided the work of early product development into much smaller batches that each delivered value independently.

In software development, user stories can deliver direct user value independently. The user value delivered by a physical product can't be broken down in the same way. Instead, we dug a little deeper to find the batches that do deliver independent value.

A Batch for Knowledge Acquisition: The Knowledge Gap

Physical product development programs deliver disappointing results when they take too long, cost too much, have reliability problems or fail to hit the market need. If these issues are discovered before product launch, they often trigger long, slow loopbacks to try to fix the problems in order to produce a viable product.

But if you want to eliminate these problems at their source, you have to go back to the decisions the team and its leaders made that introduced the problem in the first place. These can be as simple as the values entered into a set of calculations or as complex as the decision to target the wrong market first. These decisions were often made months earlier, in Early Development, when the knowledge needed to make a good decision didn't exist.

Software development teams make decisions with incomplete knowledge, too — but if a team is using Agile to organize their work into small batches, they'll find out if they're wrong right away, when the problem is easy to fix. In fact, in this environment sometimes the best thing to do is to make a "wrong decision" — aka an educated guess" — to get a reaction from the user that will point towards the right decision. As long as the feedback cycle is short, the loopbacks will be small and fast, minimizing the amount of rework.

We can do some similar things with new technologies like virtual reality and 3D printing to get faster feedback, but the distance from there to a manufacturable product is still long and complex. Most hardware teams know about these methods and increasingly use them to run experiments to explore their ideas in Early Development, but they barely scratch the surface of the overall work to be done.

Even if a team has access to the state-of-the-art tools for rapid prototyping, they are still vulnerable to making poor decisions that lead to long, slow loopbacks. Without a way to ensure they are building the knowledge they need to make better decisions, they tend to fall into a default mode of making decisions too early. They'll often fall into a cycle of "build-test-fix" loops that may result in a working prototype with a team that doesn't understand why it works or what they've learned, which means they don't know how to evolve it into the next-generation product later on.

Sometimes the team can wander around a long time in the "fuzzy front end" seeking product/market fit, and sometimes they arrive at their first system prototype only to find that some core assumptions about the technology are not true at a system level. When late-found defects and other problems crop up, the issues are deeply embedded in the system and difficult to fix.

This is where the Knowledge Gap comes in. The Rapid Learning Cycles framework defines Knowledge Gaps as clearly defined batches of the knowledge needed to make better, more confident decisions. The value delivered by the Knowledge Gap is the knowledge itself. While teams can have Knowledge Gaps about anything related to their product, the Knowledge Gaps related to high-impact/high-unknown decisions (Key Decisions) are especially valuable because they directly eliminate the root causes of long, slow loopbacks.

The next chapter will focus on the Rapid Learning Cycles framework, which uses the tools of queueing theory to optimize the flow of knowledge creation through a program so that teams experience far fewer of these, long, slow loopbacks.

A Batch for Hardware/Software Integration: The Integration Slice
We also find long, slow loopbacks in hardware/software integration. If a team waits until all hardware and software are feature-complete before

putting them together, they are highly likely to find problems in integration testing that require loopbacks to fix. To make matters worse, the test schedule is optimized for the Integration Test team, grouping unrelated tasks together to reduce labor or optimize use of scarce physical prototypes. This means that the entire test plan can get held up by a problem that didn't require the full set suite to uncover.

Chapters Five and Six will describe what happened when Kathy and her colleagues applied the insights from queueing theory to this problem. It turned out that this work could also be broken down into smaller batches, which we are calling "integration slices."

A "slice" is an identified, testable set of functionality that slices through the architecture, including both hardware and software. These slices are fairly independent of each other, although usually best delivered in a given order. Teams can organize these slices into an Integration Train that uses the tools of queueing theory to optimize the flow of these slices as the product moves towards production.

How to Achieve Agility in Physical Product Teams

Now that you know how queueing theory explains why Agile practices work for software teams — but why hardware teams don't have the same batches and queues — you're prepared to learn how to use the same principles to help your teams become faster, more flexible and responsive. In other words, more agile.

Note that these are not the principles defined by the Manifesto for Agile Software Development that have guided the development of Agile methods since 2002. Many of the Agile Manifesto principles represent a domain-specific interpretation of the fundamental principles of queueing theory, and all of them represent a response to the problems that software development teams had circa 2002. They only apply to the extent that teams have the same development system with the same batches.

It's no surprise that the attempt to use Scrum we described in Chapter One ended up in a different place by the end: We had a different system with a different set of problems to solve. Our experience then, and with all the teams we've worked with since, shows that we can increase agility — speed, flexibility and responsiveness — by using the same fundamental principles that support Agile Software Development.

We just have to acknowledge that the practices and tools will be fundamentally different in the physical world. In the rest of this book, you'll learn which practices and tools are delivering repeatable results — and *why* they work — so that you can adapt them to meet the needs of your own physical product teams.

CHAPTER THREE

Rapid Learning Cycles for Early Development

Katherine chose to call the framework that evolved in Chapter One "Rapid Learning Cycles" because the terms Scrum and Agile both led to misunderstandings, especially among people who had only seen queueing theory applied in software development. By 2014, all the organizations we mentioned in Chapter One had converged on the Rapid Learning Cycles framework, which no longer looked much like Scrum.

Today, we consider the Rapid Learning Cycles framework to be part of the agile universe — because we are using the same underlying principles and leveraging the practices to the extent they make sense. It is a distinct form of agile for optimizing workflows in areas that have both high uncertainty and high cost-of-change. The high cost-of-change distinguishes physical product development from digital product development.

Figure 3.1 shows where and when teams optimize their workflows by using traditional project tools, Agile Software Development and Rapid Learning Cycles. Traditional tools like GANTT charts work well when there is low uncertainty but high cost-of-change. These tools allow Project Managers to optimize the sequence of tasks with tools like Critical Path Analysis, and to manage complex chains of dependencies between activities and deliverables.

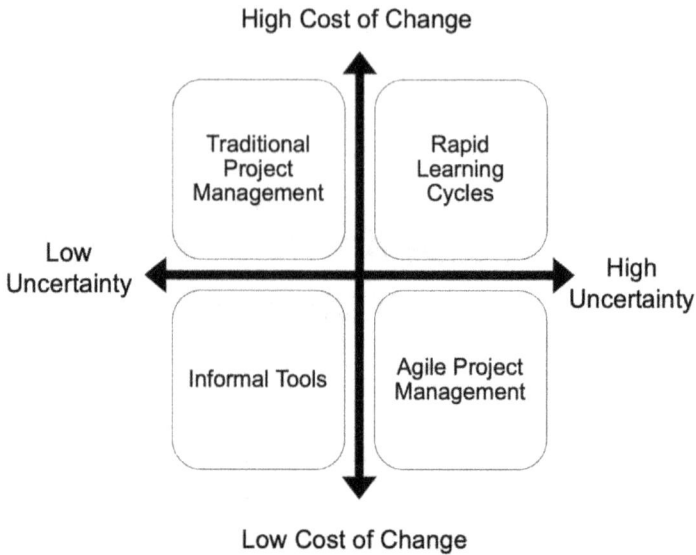

High Cost of Change

| Traditional Project Management | Rapid Learning Cycles |
| Informal Tools | Agile Project Management |

Low Uncertainty — High Uncertainty

Low Cost of Change

*Figure 3.1: The Right Tool for Project Management Depends on
Uncertainty and Cost-of-Change*

As we discussed in the last chapter, Agile works well where teams have high uncertainty but low cost-of-change. That allows them to work in small batches with rapid feedback. In fact, when cost-of-change is low, the best thing teams can do is to make "wrong" provisional decisions and then iterate on them until they are right.

Rapid Learning Cycles Optimize the Flow of Knowledge Creation

The Rapid Learning Cycles framework seeks to optimize the flow of knowledge creation through Early Development, when teams have high uncertainty and high cost-of-change. The unit of work — the batch we manage — is the Knowledge Gap. The value delivered is the knowledge created and captured to close the Knowledge Gap and inform its related Key Decision.

When we seek to optimize the flow of Knowledge Gaps, we can provide the structure, rigor and sense of urgency that the "fuzzy front end" often lacks. Research, Innovation and Concept Development teams have stronger focus and more alignment to build the knowledge leaders need to make good decisions. This eliminates long, slow loopbacks at the source. It also helps leaders optimize their product portfolio and platform roadmaps to make better use of the time, resources and capital they have to invest in innovation.

If an idea is not a good one, this process will help teams fail faster so that they can move on to other things that may be more promising. If an idea is good, teams will be positioned to accelerate it through development. They will be able to move more smoothly from Exploration to Investigation to Execution without having to loop back because a major decision didn't work out as expected.

They've eliminated the obstacles that slow down innovation programs or cause them to deliver disappointing results. They've solved many of the problems that a Product team has when they build a physical product. By optimizing the flow of knowledge creation, the entire organization gets its best ideas to market faster.

Rapid Learning Cycles Pull Stronger Innovation Practices

The Rapid Learning Cycles framework supports innovation by encouraging teams to learn earlier, before they need to make the decisions that could trigger long, slow loopbacks late in development. Figure 3.2 shows how the Rapid Learning Cycles framework breaks down innovation work into short, fast cycles of experimentation.

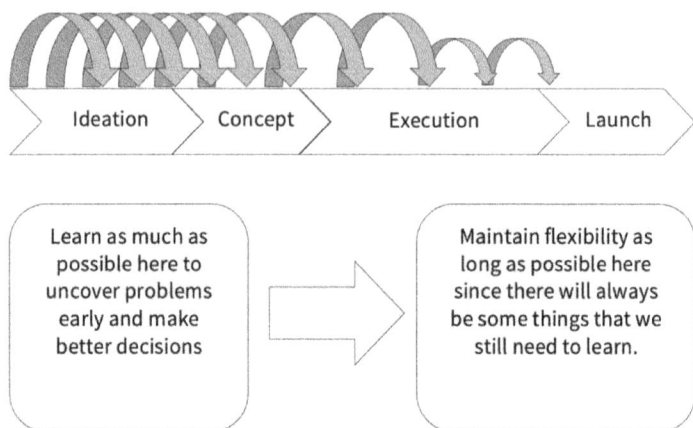

Figure 3.2: Rapid Learning Cycles in Product Development

The implementation details of the Rapid Learning Cycles framework are beyond the scope of this book. (Katherine's second book, *The Shortest Distance Between You and Your New Product*, reviews the details that an Innovation, Research or Product Development team needs to know.) Here, we'll explain why Rapid Learning Cycles help Early Development teams achieve agility, define the elements of the framework and show how these pieces fit together to accelerate innovation in the early phases of product development.

Rapid Learning Cycles Maximize the Throughput of Knowledge

Once we know that the unit of work is the Knowledge Gap, we can use ideas from Scrum and other Agile Software Development methods to optimize the flow of these Knowledge Gaps into Key Decisions. From Chapter Two, we know that we want small batches — but not too small.

The optimal batch size for a Knowledge Gap is one good, clear, crisp, focused question.

We know that we want to limit work-in-process, but since Knowledge Gaps are tied to Key Decisions that have real deadlines and complicated dependencies, we can't just throw everything into a backlog. Instead, we build a time-based plan, and then update that plan as new information comes in. Since we also want to put repeating events on a cadence, we organize this plan into regular timeboxes (called Learning Cycles) on a regular two- to four-week cadence.

A timebox is a concept that shows up again and again in the rest of the book because it's especially useful for managing knowledge work. It's a defined period of time during which a batch of work has to be finished. It's a way of limiting WIP by limiting the scope of a batch. The team works on the batch until the time is up. If it doesn't seem done, the team has to make an explicit decision whether or not to continue working — the default answer is to declare it "done enough."

Timeboxes work especially well for knowledge work because that type of work tends to expand to fill the available time. For example, a team may have the Knowledge Gap: "Which suppliers make the material we need?" A person could take an hour to search the internet, a few days to interview suppliers, a few weeks to visit suppliers or a few months to acquire and test samples. How much detail does the team need right now? How much time do they want to invest in this question, relative to other questions? Timeboxes limit the team's investment in the work.

This is especially important in Early Development because every team we have ever encountered has more they could learn than they have time to learn. If they were allowed unlimited time, they might never finish. Instead, we ruthlessly prioritize these Knowledge Gaps, even admitting from the start that some low-priority Knowledge Gaps won't be closed at all.

Learning Cycles Pull Learning Forward and Push Decisions Later

It takes time to build up the knowledge a team needs to make its most important decisions. To find its Knowledge Gaps and Key Decisions, teams look for their NUDs (New, Unique, Difficult areas of the product). The project's NUDs don't just highlight Knowledge Gaps. They also point to the areas where the team's instincts are more likely to lead them astray. The Knowledge Gaps expose the "known unknowns," but NUDs also have "unknown unknowns."

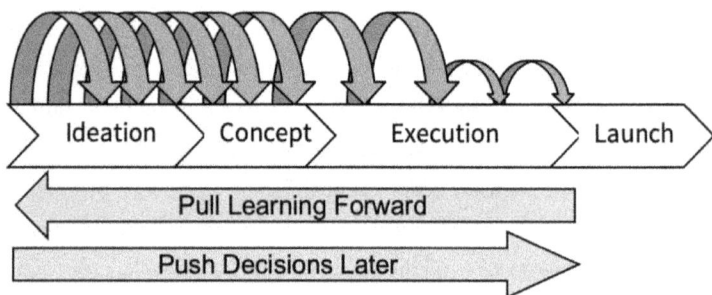

Figure 3.3: Teams Running Rapid Learning Cycles Pull Learning Forward and Push Decisions Later

Figure 3.3 shows that the Rapid Learning Cycles framework encourages teams to pull learning forward — to close Knowledge Gaps early. It also encourages them to push decisions later — all the way to the "Last Responsible Moment," an idea Katherine first encountered in 2002 with Mary Poppendieck's work exploring the connections between Agile Software Development and Lean Manufacturing.

The Last Responsible Moment for a decision is the final point in time to make a decision before you begin impacting the people downstream of you. Decisions made before this point in time can still be changed without making anyone too upset or bothered. Decisions made after this point in time can be prohibitively expensive and put the launch schedule at risk.

Waiting until the Last Responsible Moment is difficult to do in most companies, especially in the United States, where we Americans have a bias towards acting quickly and decisively. But it is the secret to faster innovation because it keeps teams from making the kinds of missteps that only slow them down right when they can least afford to go slower. It allows time for the "unknown unknowns" to rise to the surface.

In Katherine's experience, major decisions that get made too early often get revisited, sometimes much later than the Last Responsible Moment. In fact, this is the root cause behind a lot of project delays, cost overruns and disappointing results. Such challenges aren't anyone's fault; the team just didn't have the knowledge it needed when the decision makers made the decision. Sometimes these decisions get revisited because new information came to light, and sometimes they get revisited because they are the only places where things can still flex to fix problems in other areas.

When a major decision gets made, other decisions and deliverables get built around it. If that major decision is revisited, all that interrelated work has to be redone, adding time and cost to the program. When a team holds a major decision open, however, that work gets set aside while the team focuses on the parts of the system that are more certain. When the team finalizes the decision, the other things around it can be finalized, too, with all of it much less likely to shift.

Of course, delaying decisions also gives the team more time to learn about the decision so that it can be made using the best available information at the time. The learning inside Rapid Learning Cycles is focused on making these decisions with greater confidence.

The Elements of Rapid Learning Cycles Are Built Around Learning

The central element of the Rapid Learning Cycles framework is the learning cycle. As we showed in Chapter Two, we optimize workflows by putting regular events on a cadence. The learning cycle establishes the cadence that ties the whole system together.

This short, focused period of work — the timebox — seeks to answer questions the team has about an aspect of their project so that they can make better decisions. During a learning cycle, team members build knowledge to help answer these questions, and then at the end of a learning cycle they share what they've learned with their teams, then decide what to learn next.

They end with an event during which team members get to show their recent work and replan their next cycle of work. The team uses a visual planning board to organize their plan, using whiteboards with sticky notes (or virtual online planning tools). These sticky notes contain the batches of knowledge — Knowledge Gaps and Key Decisions that are flowing through the Development team.

Because the team's focus is on knowledge creation, the team must be aligned around the overall project direction before they start. Each Rapid Learning Cycles project begins with a Kickoff Event to build this alignment. The first task of a Kickoff Event is to define the team's Core Hypothesis.

The Core Hypothesis Defines the Product

Katherine added the Core Hypothesis to the framework after observing that teams with a "product mission statement" or "product vision" spent less time arguing about fundamental things like "What's the business model?" or "Who is the real customer for this?" The Core Hypothesis ensures that the team is aligned around the project's basic assumptions about technology, customer and business value, and is therefore able to recognize when the assumptions have been validated or when they are no longer true.

The Core Hypothesis is a short description of the product vision that the team develops during one of their first meetings together. It's developed as a team so that all team members are aligned about the product's most important objectives. It describes the reasons why the team believes this idea will create customer and business value.

Here is a real Core Hypothesis from Agersens, a startup that developed a virtual fencing system for livestock: "The eShepherd is a full virtual fencing solution from the collar to the app that eliminates the need for physical fences as it provides better information about the location of each member of a herd to increase production and lower costs so that we grow Agersens into profitability."

This example includes the product (virtual fencing) that will deliver customer value (increase production and lower costs) and business value (growth) with enough specificity to give direction but without over-constraining the solution.

The Core Hypothesis points the team towards some of the most important early learning they can do: Develop better knowledge about the concept's soundness as a product. The team will either validate the assumptions embedded in the Core Hypothesis or demonstrate that the product concept has some fundamental flaws before the company spends much time and money on it.

The Core Hypothesis may change as the team deepens its understanding of the product, customers and markets. In fact, if it's a truly new idea, the Core Hypothesis often changes a lot as the team learns more about potential customers and markets. But it should not drift. When it changes, the program team and all the stakeholders need to know not only that it changed but also why, so that they all get realigned on the project's new direction.

The Core Hypothesis plays such a central role that teams often assume it must come from above — that leadership should define it. But

Katherine coaches Project Leaders to make sure their teams develop this statement themselves. This way, any misunderstandings or other misalignments will come to the surface where they can be addressed right away. Fifteen minutes of extra discussion here can save fifteen days' worth of time lost to a misunderstanding between subsystem owners.

Key Decisions Drive Product Success

In Chapter One, we described how the concept of the Key Decision came to play an important role in the framework. We said that a Key Decision is a significant decision that has high impact on a product's ultimate success, and that the team does not have the knowledge to make with confidence. Innovation teams handle these decisions carefully because they make or break the program.

If a Knowledge Gap is a cookie and a Learning Cycle is a batch of cookies, the Key Decision is the cookie plate you arrange to bring to the party. It's where all of the Knowledge Gaps come together to deliver value, even if you have different types of cookies baked at different times on the same plate. To Agile Software Development experts, this may sound like an epic, but we'll describe later why that's not a good analogy.

An Innovation team will make thousands of decisions before the product launches or the process goes live. But not all those decisions have the same importance. Some are relatively easy to change later. Others affect only a small part of the system. These low-impact decisions don't need special attention because if the team gets one of these wrong, they can either change it or it won't matter in the end. Key Decisions are the ones that the team needs to get right the first time, or the product will go on a long detour.

High Impact
on the Business Case

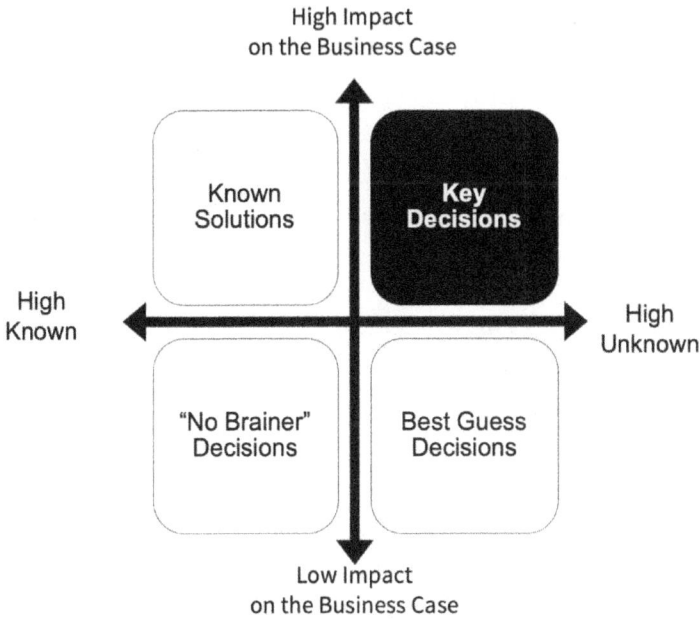

High
Known

High
Unknown

Known
Solutions

Key
Decisions

"No Brainer"
Decisions

Best Guess
Decisions

Low Impact
on the Business Case

Figure 3.4: Key Decisions Are High-Impact/High-Unknown Decisions

Figure 3.4 shows how we decide whether or not a decision is a Key Decision. Other decisions leverage known solutions. Many arise naturally out of the team's experience and the knowledge readily available to them. Some decisions get imposed on a team by technology or market constraints. Key Decisions are the ones that enable the product to do something new, unique or different than previous products.

You can find your program's Key Decisions by asking, "What's new, unique or difficult about this program?" These NUDs are, by definition, Key Decisions. They can come from the technical side, the commercial side, or from places like Legal or Regulatory Affairs. You can find other Key Decisions by looking for decisions that rise to the same level as your NUDs in terms of both impact on the project and lack of knowledge needed to make the decision.

Key Decisions have a sequence that reflects the process for executing the innovation. When teams understand how Key Decisions flow into one another, the sequence and timing for these decisions and who is ultimately responsible for making the decisions, they will be better prepared to make these decisions with confidence at the right time. And the decisions are much less likely to be revisited, which helps the entire program run at higher velocity.

Knowledge Gaps Highlight Learning to Be Done

A Knowledge Gap is something the decision maker needs to know in order to make a Key Decision with confidence. Since Chapter One, we've defined this as the "batch of work" that gets managed: Knowledge Gaps get assigned owners, prioritized and tracked as they close. Knowledge Gap owners produce short reports to capture what they've learned to be able to close a Knowledge Gap, and this gets incorporated into the related Key Decision recommendation.

By definition, every Key Decision has at least one Knowledge Gap to close before the decision can be made. When the team creates the first-pass list of Knowledge Gaps, they turn to their map of Key Decisions to identify the Knowledge Gaps related to those decisions. These Knowledge Gaps drive the team's work through the early phases and help the team continue to eliminate risk and integrate new information in later phases.

Innovation and Product Development teams always have more Knowledge Gaps to close than they can close. Much of the art of leading a Rapid Learning Cycles program is using systematic methods to prioritize which Knowledge Gaps to close early, which ones to defer and which ones to consciously leave open. While the prioritization process itself is beyond the scope of this book, we explicitly use concepts from Chapter Two to optimize the flow of Knowledge Gaps and organize them into learning cycles.

Knowledge Gaps are closed when the Knowledge Gap owner writes a Knowledge Gap report — a short summary of what they've learned and what they recommend as next steps. That report captures the knowledge they've built for their current team and for future teams who may encounter similar gaps. They'll share that report at a Learning Cycle Event.

Deliverables Encapsulate Decisions

Deliverables are the final outcomes of an innovation and include the product or new process itself. In the early phases, the deliverable can be as simple as a Concept Proposal that fleshes out the idea enough that it can be compared with others. In middle development, deliverables include things like proof-of-concepts, draft execution plans and budgets, business case analyses. The final phases are primarily about producing the deliverables that bring the idea to life: manufacturing tools, marketing collateral and changes to process documentation.

Both traditional and Agile program management focus on completing deliverables: requirements documents and other tasks for traditional program management and user stories for Agile Software Development. With Rapid Learning Cycles, the deliverable is the way that a Development team communicates its decisions to partners. Instead of focusing on producing these deliverables, the focus is on understanding the Key Decision sequence and then managing the work to close Knowledge Gaps so that the deliverables get produced on time and won't need to be revisited.

Learning Cycle and Integration Events Pull Real-Time Knowledge Capture

At the end of every learning cycle, teams have Learning Cycle Events to share what they've learned. When it's time to make Key Decisions, teams have Integration Events to bring together the decision makers with the knowledge the team has built to close the decisions. Both events pull the work of innovation by building urgency and accountability into the process as they drive real-time knowledge capture. Figure 3.5 shows how this works within a phase of development.

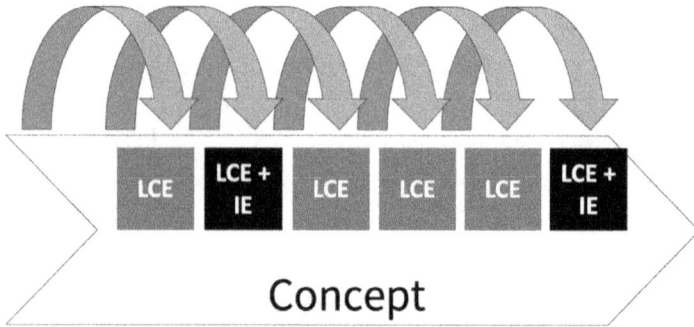

Figure 3.5: Each Learning Cycle Concludes with a Pull Event

Knowledge work tends to expand to fill the available time, so Innovation Teams place a strict limit on that time before requiring team members to share what they have learned.

Every learning cycle is a timebox: a fixed amount of time that the team will use to learn as much as it can about its Knowledge Gaps. Within that time, team members can structure their work in any way that will maximize learning. This is how the framework applies WIP limits and optimal batch sizes.

Integration Events not only serve as the focus for getting clear decisions. They also keep innovation sponsors engaged and informed about the true state of the programs they sponsor. The innovation sponsors and other stakeholders get a chance to see the team learning in real-time, provide feedback on the team's Key Decisions and Knowledge Gaps, and review the results of their experimentation.

Teams Leverage Agile Practices That Make Sense

Agile Software Development teams have been managing regular cadences of events for a long time, and the Rapid Learning Cycles framework borrows the practices that make sense while discarding everything else.

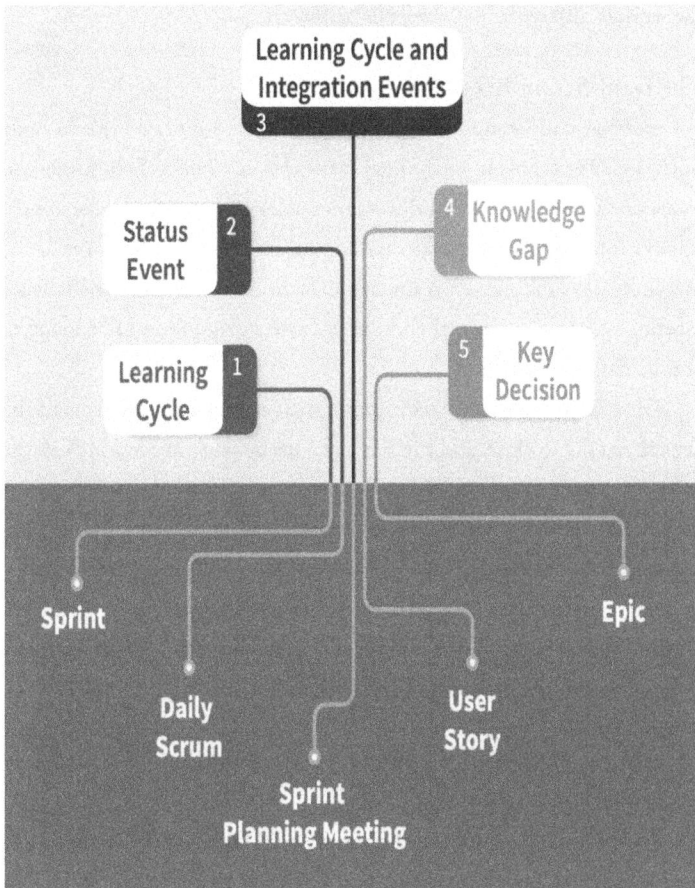

Figure 3.6: The Agile Roots of the Rapid Learning Cycles Framework

If you're familiar with Scrum, you'll see in Figure 3.6 that Katherine adapted the elements of the Scrum framework in specific ways. The use of new terms is intentional; a lot of teams partner with software teams that use Scrum, and a few have even tried Scrum or other variants of Agile themselves. Katherine's found that it's much less confusing for everyone when Rapid Learning Cycles uses different terms because the nature of the work is different.

The Daily Scrum Is Too Often

For example, daily standup meetings play a key coordination role in Agile Software Development — so important that the entire Scrum method was named for the daily scrum at its center. These scrums provide opportunities for problems to surface and for a team member who's overloaded to get help from another team member. Software teams benefit from meeting every day because their batches (user stories) are small enough to require daily coordination.

Knowledge Gaps are usually larger than a user story, in terms of the time they take to close, and there is not a lot of value in breaking out the tasks to close a Knowledge Gap for anyone except the Knowledge Gap owner. They benefit from the opportunity to talk about what they are doing, surface problems and ask for help, but the work to close Knowledge Gaps has a slower pace. A daily stand-up can get frustrating — it can seem like nothing's moving. Teams usually do better with a Status Event two or three times per week instead of a daily scrum.

Learning Cycle Events Capture Value at the End of a Learning Cycle

The most important difference between Rapid Learning Cycles and Agile Software Development, on a practical level, occurs at the end of a learning cycle. Agile methods often advocate for a Demo to show the software that was built during a sprint. A Demo is the best way to get immediate feedback on the just-completed software. This immediate feedback is a big part of the value delivered by the sprint.

When a physical product team tries to use Agile Software Development methods directly, they will try to have Demos, and they will sometimes even build special prototypes for these events. But a demo prototype that's disconnected from the team's flow of Knowledge Gaps is wasted effort. It doesn't effectively demonstrate the progress the team is making because the hardware team is not building the product as a series of independent batches of work.

Hardware teams can and should get feedback on their concepts, but it's better done as part of the process of closing specific Knowledge Gaps or making specific Key Decisions. The team's ability to make Key Decisions at the Last Responsible Moment is a much better demonstration of progress. Our experience shows that this metric predicts on-time delivery in Early Development better than any other measure.

Instead of making demos, we ask teams to write short summaries of the knowledge they've created in the form of one-page Knowledge Gap Reports. These reports go directly to Key Decision owners and decision makers to help inform their decisions. At the end of a learning cycle, Knowledge Gap owners share their Knowledge Gap reports with each other. At Integration Events, also done at the end of a learning cycle and usually after the Learning Cycle Event, teams share these reports with decision makers and other stakeholders to inform Key Decisions.

Learning Cycle Plans Instead of Backlogs

After a software team conducts a Demo, they plan for the next sprint by pulling user stories out of their backlog, pruning the backlog of user stories no longer needed and reprioritizing the backlog. This makes sense for them because their user stories are independent: They can choose the next user stories that make the most sense at the start of the sprint, and they will complete these user stories before the end of the sprint. This planning process usually takes much longer than the Demo.

As we described in Chapter One, this didn't make sense at all for Knowledge Gaps. Instead, we use a time-based plan that maps Knowledge Gaps into learning cycles in advance, so we can make sure we're building the knowledge needed to make upcoming Key Decisions. We build this plan during a Kickoff Event at the start of the process.

After a physical product team holds their Learning Cycle Event, they also replan. However, they will not have to start with an empty learning cycle. They will have Knowledge Gaps from the previous learning cycle that have not closed. They will have pre-planned some Knowledge Gaps to start based on when the related Key Decision needs to be made. They will have to add new Knowledge Gaps and may need to move others to balance resources. There is no backlog to prune or reprioritize. All of this will take much less time than they'll need to share their Knowledge Gap reports and make Key Decisions.

Key Decisions Are Not Epics

When Agile Software Development experts look at the Rapid Learning Cycles framework, they often assume that the relationship between a Key Decision and a Knowledge Gap is the same as the relationship between an epic and a user story. An epic is a collection of user stories but a Key Decision is not a collection of Knowledge Gaps.

For one thing, an epic cannot be done until all of its related user stories are done, but we make Key Decisions at the Last Responsible Moment with the best available knowledge. If some Knowledge Gaps aren't done, the team usually makes the decision anyway, accepting the risk of the unclosed Knowledge Gaps.

Most Agile tools assume a one-to-many relationship between epics and user stories. A given user story may be assigned to one and only one epic. But Knowledge Gaps can inform multiple Key Decisions, and it's important to understand all of these dependencies.

Activities and Deliverables Are Not User Stories

Katherine occasionally gets called upon to do "Agile Rescue Missions" for teams that have attempted to use Agile for a physical product and gotten themselves so stuck that nothing is moving at all. This usually happens because teams — and their naïve Agile coaches — have attempted to define the team's activities and deliverables as user stories.

When they do that, teams find that their backlogs blow up, and that sprint planning takes longer and longer. If the team's also been encouraged to run two-week cycles, the amount of overhead — the transaction cost incurred by the sprint itself — gets bigger and bigger. Katherine has encountered teams that were spending more than 25 percent of their total capacity on basically admin work to split large activities into small ones, and then manage all of these small bits.

Once a team is further along, in the Execution phases of delivery, there is a way to do this that makes sense, and we'll talk about that in Chapter Four. But this way of working is not at all appropriate for the learning phases of early product development, when the team's focus is on building knowledge. Instead, teams assign owners and deadlines for major deliverables and manage them at the level of Key Decisions without breaking things down further.

Rapid Learning Cycles Pull Better Decisions

Rapid Learning Cycles drives the team to ask, "What do we already know, and what knowledge do we need to make this decision?" The process helps teams think more deeply about decisions. Before going into an Integration Event, they ask themselves, "Is it really the right time for us to make this decision? Are we at that Last Responsible Moment?" Teams that have the answer to this question are prepared to be flexible and responsive — they have achieved agility.

CHAPTER FOUR

Fast, Flexible Flow in the Middle Phases of Development

B y 2015, Katherine had built the Rapid Learning Cycles framework into an innovation project management system that delivered repeatable results. Teams would get through those early phases knowing that they had made better, more confident decisions, and then ask the guiding question, "What do we do now?"

Within the Rapid Learning Cycles user community, we have companies that manage their projects strictly as a hybrid of Rapid Learning Cycles with traditional tools like GANTT charts and risk registers in later phases. Our most advanced user community members — the ones who have fully adopted Rapid Learning Cycles and continue to expand it — have found ways to continue to optimize their workflows through the middle and late phases of development. This chapter and the next two describe how we can sustain speed, flexibility and responsiveness as the deadline for release-to-production draws closer.

The Challenge in the Middle Phases of Physical Product Development

Most product development teams use traditional project management tools for managing Detailed Design and later phases. This makes sense because Rapid Learning Cycles has reduced the risk and lowered the uncertainty, reducing the amount of change the team needs to accommodate. At the same time, it becomes much more important to manage dependencies and ensure that all affected parties get notified when things do change. Traditional tools accommodate those needs.

But that doesn't mean the plan is as stable as the plan to build a house. In middle development, teams still have learning to do, but the team's focus is more on producing the deliverables that their partners need to produce the product at scale, sell it and support it in the field. While the team still has some Key Decisions to make and Knowledge Gaps to close, their focus turns more towards executing decisions that have already been made.

The team still needs planning methods that can optimize flow when the path to production still has unknowns. The team still needs to get rapid feedback, especially when subsystems get put together for the first time. The team also now needs to integrate practices like design reviews that will help them avoid preventable mistakes when executing the team's decisions without letting teams get bogged down with too many checklist items.

Phases and Gates in Product Development

Both Kathy and Katherine spent years inside HP's printer divisions, which had product development processes (PDPs) based on phases and gates. Since then, almost all of their clients also have phase-gate PDPs. Figure 4.1 shows how a typical phase-gate PDP is structured.

Periodically, Agile or Lean experts grow skeptical of phase-gate PDPs because they look like they enforce traditional waterfall development, with all the long, slow loopbacks that implies. Neither of us would ever suggest that software programs need phase-gates if they have a well-run Agile process.

Phase Gate Product Development Process

> Concept > Feasibility > Design > Industrialize > Launch >

Phases
(sometimes
called Stages)

Gates

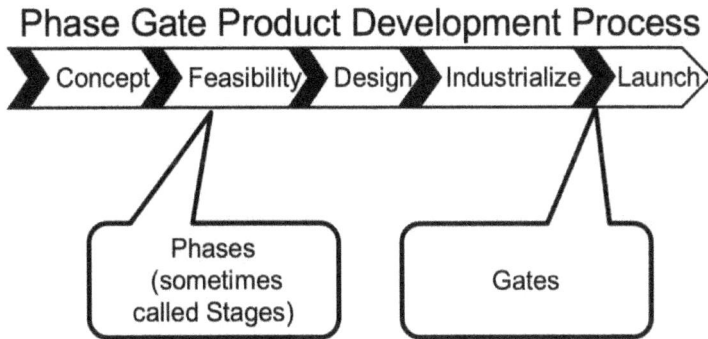

Figure 4.1: A Typical Phase-Gate Product Development Process

But our experience has shown that healthy phase-gates are essential for effective physical product development because of the escalating levels of investment and business commitment required to go from idea to launch.

There are plenty of unhealthy phase-gate PDPs out there that have become swollen with too many inflexible deliverables that drive teams to make decisions too early, and to jump into Execution without knowing enough to make good decisions. But the problem is not the structure of a phase-gate PDP. The problem is that the organization is using the structure as a means of enforcing practices and tools within the PDP that don't make sense for every team. A Gate Review in this type of PDP can be a rubber stamp or a detailed audit or anything in between. But it's not a healthy discussion around the business need for the product in development.

Since Project Team Leaders usually have a good eye for the deliverables that could be jettisoned from a program, they steer the team away from those. In the worst cases, these deliverables get done in a slapdash manner right before the gate, put in a drawer and never seen again. In this way, the Project Team Leader reduces — but can't entirely eliminate

— the waste of producing these unnecessary deliverables. All of this takes away from the business decisions that lie at the center of a healthy phase-gate PDP.

Healthy phase-gate PDPs focus Gate Reviews on the business decision of whether or not to invest in the next phase of development. They weigh factors like expected ROI and strategic fit against the cost of the remaining phases of development. If the market has shifted or the product is too expensive to produce despite the best efforts of the team, the product can and probably should be stopped here.

Healthy phase-gates also have checklists, but they're tailored to fit the needs of individual programs — and Gate Reviews are not default deadlines for most of them. Instead, the Gate Reviews focus on questions around acceptable levels of risk, strategic alignment and business value. The deliverables for the Gate Review are fewer in number and take less time to put together but contain essential information for helping leaders ask and answer these questions.

It's possible to have a great product that doesn't pass a gate because it no longer fits with the strategy for the product line. It's possible to have an immature product pass a gate with a higher-than-usual level of risk because accelerating this product to market is worth the risk and the business is willing to accept the consequences of a late failure.

The Rapid Learning Cycles framework slots naturally into the first one, two or three phases of these PDPs, which typically focus on screening ideas, developing concepts and assessing feasibility. In the context of a phase-gate PDP, we run Rapid Learning Cycles within a phase, and the primary goal is to develop the knowledge needed to help the business leaders make good decisions at the gate. Figure 4.2 shows how this works.

The Key Decisions and deliverables are all built around the needs for the Gate Review. The target date for the next gate determines the length of the Learning Cycles Plan. After the team passes through the gate, they hold a new Kickoff Event to establish the Learning Cycles Plan for the next phase of work.

Phase Gate Product Development Process

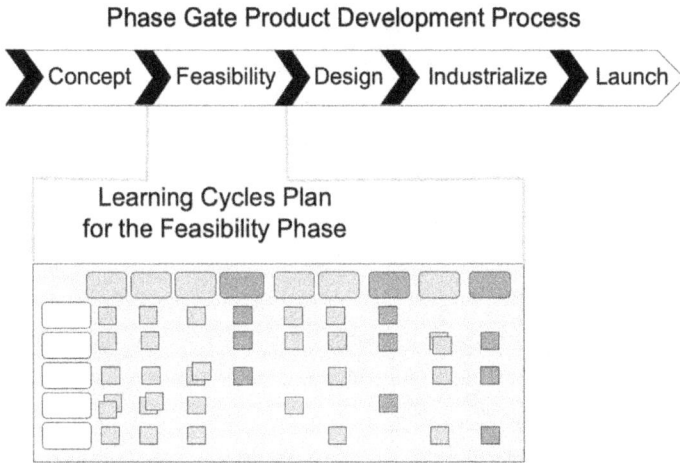

Figure 4.2: The Learning Cycles Plan for The Feasibility Phase

The looming question about the later phases — the Execution phases of Detailed Product and Process Design, Industrialization, and Launch — is how to sustain speed, flexibility and responsiveness as the product itself matures.

Four Opportunities to Preserve Agility in Middle and Late Development

The closer the project team gets to production, the more constrained they'll be by the work that's already been done on their project. Here are four ways to preserve the flexibility they do have for as long as possible without adding cost and while continuing to eliminate risk:

- Continue to make Key Decisions at the Last Responsible Moment and seek to delay that moment as long as possible. This allows teams more time to build knowledge and more time for new information to develop. It preserves flexibility so that the team has room to maneuver if something unexpected happens.

- Prevent long, slow loopbacks, driven by mistakes in the Execution phase, by shortening the feedback cycles. This is the purpose of a design review: to spot problems within a design before it's even built into a prototype. Every deliverable produced by the team needs to have such short cycles of feedback.

- Preserve flexibility in high-risk areas of the system with convergence: the pursuit of multiple alternatives for solving a design problem to increase the likelihood that the team will find a solution that works within the time they have, and to delay the Last Responsible Moment for decisions even longer to preserve flexibility.

- Plan and organize the flow of work to accommodate the dynamic nature of these development phases.

When teams use Rapid Learning Cycles in Early Development, it's natural to continue the structure as the project moves into the Execution phases. The companies that have fully adopted Rapid Learning Cycles often do just that: They keep the structure and time-based plan of Rapid Learning Cycles as their focus shifts towards execution. In Katherine's most recent work, she's started to call these "execution cycles" as shown in Figure 4.3.

While this may look similar to other approaches like SAFe® or Modified Agile for Hardware Development, it differs in four important ways:

- We do not attempt to establish a single goal for these cycles — a specific piece of functionality that will be delivered — until we are near the end and actually have full system prototypes. We'll cover those late phases of development in Chapters Five and Six.

- We do not call a cycle an "iteration" or an "increment" because the deliverables being done within an execution cycle are not shippable on their own and don't add up to a working product. Instead, we optimize what gets done based on lead times.

Phase Gate Product Development Process

> Concept > Feasibility > Design > Industrialize > Launch >

Execution Cycles Plan
for the Design Phase

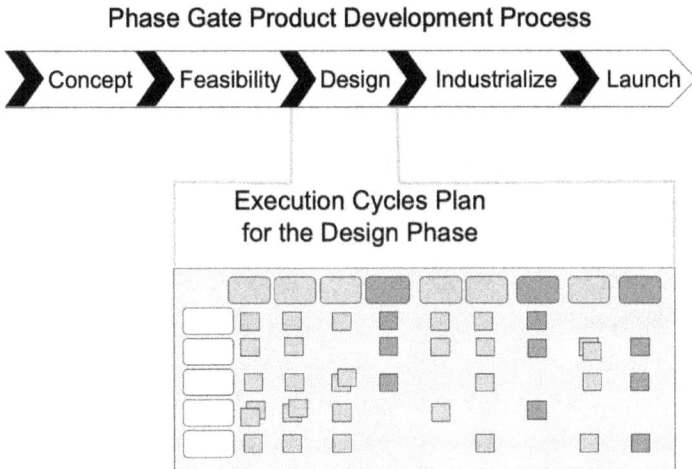

Figure 4.3: The Execution Cycles Plan for the Design Phase

- While we map out the cycles only as far ahead as we can see, we do not maintain a backlog, break down deliverables into smaller tasks or attempt to convert them to user stories or "program increments." None of these things make sense in the context of a physical product.

- The Project Leader creates a GANTT chart covering the rest of the program through launch, and this GANTT chart drives how deliverables are assigned to execution cycles.

Execution cycles allow teams to get the benefits of working in a regular cadence, cutting batch sizes and limiting WIP. They don't use Agile Software Development constructs that are not helpful when there are dependencies, long lead times, and resources from a variety of specific disciplines to manage with high cost-of-change. They don't start over with a new plan every sprint or program increment.

Deliverables Drive Execution Cycles

The team defines a set of deliverables (including unclosed Knowledge Gaps) to complete in an execution cycle. They continue to conduct Integration Events to help them make Key Decisions and finalize major deliverables. Just as a Knowledge Gap is not done until the knowledge has been captured in a Knowledge Gap Report, a deliverable is not done until it has been tested (or at least reviewed) to uncover issues that could cause trouble later.

The term "deliverable" is intentionally broad. Physical product teams have to produce a variety of things to take a product into production, and these things differ by the type of product. Mechanical products need CAD models. Electrical products need layouts for PCBAs. Chemical products need formulations. For a biological product, the deliverables may include an organism that contains the genetic code needed to make a protein.

All of these products also need sufficient requirements and specifications to develop good validation test plans. Some need specific deliverables to meet regulatory requirements around health and safety or to comply with industry standards.

Each of these deliverables needs an owner — a person who is responsible for getting it done — and a process for providing fast feedback on that deliverable, such as a design review.

A team using execution cycles will populate the plan with the remaining Key Decisions and Knowledge Gaps. They will also plan their deliverables and milestones. They may have things like CAD models, approved RFPs, purchase orders for prototype parts and the prototype builds themselves in the plan.

The goal is to reach the first full system prototype with a product design that can move smoothly into commercialization, with few loopbacks to rework it, only minor problems to fix and very low risk that a problem will emerge after the product is out in the field.

Typical Hardware Development Increases Risk

In a typical hardware development program, teams develop specifications, then turn those into CAD models and eventually physical prototypes. The specifications, CAD models and prototypes contain a collection of decisions that will not be fully validated until the first full system prototype, and sometimes not until the first production run.

Some aspects of development lend themselves to low-resolution prototypes that look nothing like the final product: breadboards used to evaluate circuit designs or concept drawings used to validate industrial design direction. Other aspects require a more realistic prototype because they depend more on the interaction of different parts of the system: total size and weight, total cost, feedback from early users. But many product development teams use their full system prototypes for everything, uncovering things in these prototypes that could have been found earlier.

The typical test strategy exacerbates this. The team organizes tests to minimize the number of prototypes needed because these objects are expensive. The tests assume that all or most of the requirements have been implemented by the time the tests start. The team then groups tests together into suites of tests that serve multiple purposes, combining things like reliability testing with functional testing on the same unit. If a feature hasn't been implemented yet, it can block the rest of the test suite. If a problem is discovered, the team has to go back into design to fix the problem and then re-run the test suite, making these loopbacks even longer.

As Figure 4.4 shows, *this* is waterfall development, and it is inherently bad. When validation is delayed until the end, teams don't learn about problems until they've already become expensive and time-consuming to fix. This increases the risk of a project delay or cost overrun. The later the problem is found, the higher the risk of a major project disruption.

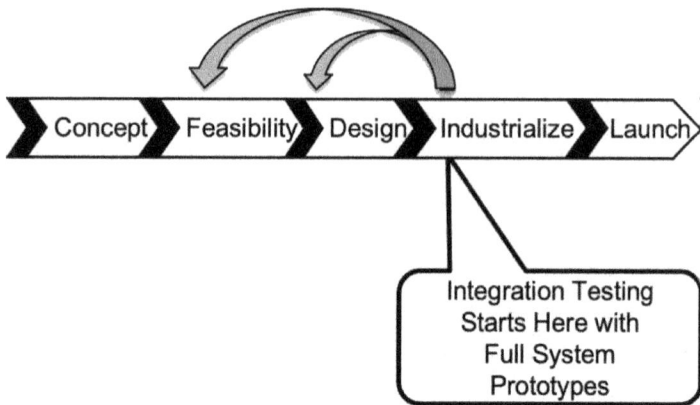

Figure 4.4: Waterfall Development

Reduce Risk in Middle Development to Smooth Out Late Development

If Early Development is all about making better decisions to set up the teams for success in middle and late development, then middle development is all about reducing risk of mistakes when these decisions are executed.

There will still be some Key Decisions and Knowledge Gaps floating around — the temptation will be to just close them already. But we've previously explained why Key Decisions taken too early increase the risk of long, slow loopbacks. Teams should continue to make these decisions at the Last Responsible Moment. For these later decisions, the timing is probably dictated by the prototype and production schedules.

In addition to managing the risk of revisiting Key Decisions, teams also now need to reduce the risk of errors introduced in the normal course of product and process design. The team needs to produce its deliverables in small batches that get validated as soon as possible after they have been created. "Validation" doesn't mean absolute proof. It may not be possible to demonstrate that a subsystem design works until the entire system prototype has been tested.

However, that doesn't mean that the product development team can do nothing. If Integration Test finds a problem, we want that problem to be something only they could have found. Peer reviews and expert reviews are just one example of faster, cheaper ways to uncover problems before they reach the first system prototypes or production runs. Figure 4.5 shows how such risk reduction activities eliminate long, slow loopbacks.

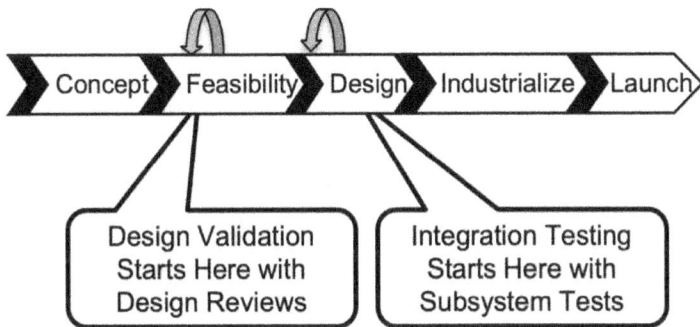

Figure 4.5: Risk Reduction Eliminates Long, Slow Loopbacks

This is a good place for checklists to help reviewers look for common problems, for design reviews and design-for-X (DfX) analyses to spot issues early, and for error-checking routines in CAD programs. Many groups already have requirements for Failure Modes and Effects Analysis (FMEA) or DfX Reviews (e.g., Design for Manufacturing) to get feedback from downstream partners.

As we saw in Chapter Two, this work could be done as one large batch at the end, but it's much more effective when it's done continuously, as batches of deliverables are completed. The extra overhead of these smaller reviews is more than made up by the reduction in the amount of time it takes to find problems in the later stages.

It's also a place to use rapid prototyping tools to provide early validation in the physical space — but Katherine has seen both good and bad uses of these tools. A team using rapid prototyping methods well is a team using rapid prototyping to build knowledge and validate subsystem-level decisions. Too many teams let rapid prototyping degrade into build-test-fix cycles that burn a lot of resources with no certainty that a solution will ever be found.

Emulators and Simulators to Shorten Feedback Loops

We've both spent a lot of time working with printers, which are bundles of hardware, software and firmware. That was a target-rich space for developing emulators and simulators to decouple the subsystems so they could be developed independently without increasing the risk of failed integration. For example, HP Laserjet circa 2010 used an emulator with a physical controller board and software that simulated printer behavior. The physical element provided realistic response timing to ensure that the emulator represented real-time behavior.

The work to build these systems is not trivial, but it has high, immediate return-on-investment by helping teams accelerate integration to shorten feedback loops, uncover problems early and save time in late development.

When a hardware team begins the work of Detailed Design, it's hard for them to effectively model the inputs and outputs from other parts of the system. If the product involves firmware (and especially in Internet-of-Things applications), the software team needs some way to validate their work before the responses from actual hardware are available.

Simulators model behaviors from subsystems through the full system in virtual space — including user behavior. An emulator is a physical device that imitates the behavior of one subsystem, providing realistic inputs and outputs so that another subsystem can be developed independently.

These systems give the team the opportunity to explore alternatives less expensively and get early feedback without having to invest in physical prototypes. For example, a software team can provide a test harness that simulates all the intended responses from software so that the hardware team can see whether or not the hardware is delivering good inputs and is responding correctly to various outputs from the firmware.

Simulators and emulators help teams evolve different parts of a system independently so they can test subsystem behavior before the full system exists. This helps them find problems early. When the team brings the full system together, they will probably still find some problems, but these will be the emergent problems that arise from full system effects. The team will not be blocked because a subsystem fails to behave as expected in its interaction with other parts of a system.

Set-Based Design and Convergence to Address High-Risk Areas

For those aspects of the design that are high risk because they are entirely new and unproven, teams can choose to reduce this risk by exploring multiple alternatives. This allows them to delay the Last Responsible Moment for the final decision to preserve flexibility, and to learn faster about the alternatives so they are more likely to find the one that best meets their needs. Figure 4.6 shows what a convergence process looks like.

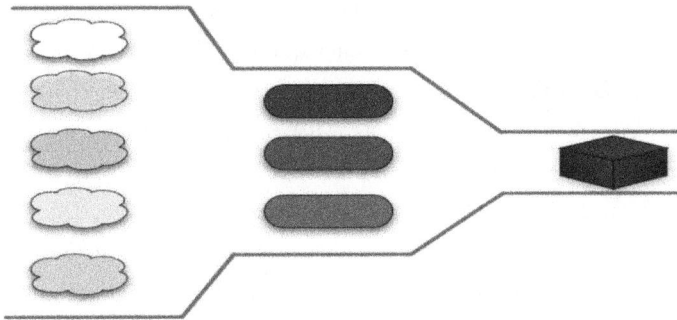

Figure 4.6: Convergence

This is not designing systems in parallel. This is a process of identifying different options for how to solve a design challenge, then explicitly testing the set of options to understand their strengths and weaknesses. As options prove to be nonviable, they get eliminated from the set. Over a series of these tests, the team reduces the number of options until they arrive at the option that works best. Often this option is a combination of the best aspects of earlier options.

Ideally, the team would delay the final decision until after a full system prototype. They can make prototype variants or design the product so that the best remaining options can be easily swapped during testing. Sometimes they'll even carry more than one option into prototype production runs, but usually the final decision takes place based on the lead times for the tooling and sourcing needed for this first pilot production run.

When teams use convergence to manage areas of high risk, they find that this preserves flexibility without driving up time or cost. The testing to understand the differences between the options builds a lot of knowledge about trade-offs and limits. This knowledge can guide decision making for the team both now and for future products, accelerating future development even more. The team can uncover problems with favored options that might have not emerged until much later in a traditional process. They may also uncover opportunities, especially when they combine the strengths of several options into one.

If the team gets all the way to the Last Responsible Moment without a clear winner among the options (and especially if there is no option at all that meets all the requirements), they have a much stronger base of knowledge to help them overcome the issues, and a much earlier warning that there is a problem that needs a resolution.

Whether the team finds the answer among the original options, creates a stronger option, or discovers that they need new alternatives, this process will help the teams make a good decision with much less risk of triggering long loopbacks.

Prototype Builds Validate Integration

A team seeking to preserve speed, flexibility and responsiveness thinks of prototypes differently than a traditional hardware team. For teams seeking agility, a prototype is only worthwhile if it answers questions about the design. It's much more than a milestone or deliverable.

The key question to answer about any prototype is "What do I want to learn?" Prototypes validate the earlier decisions and design work, so often what we want to learn is this: "How well are the different parts working together?" and "Are we on target to meet our specifications and requirements?" If there's a faster, better, cheaper way to learn those things, then it's not yet time for a full system prototype.

In queueing theory, a full system prototype is a batch — and usually a large one! If the team is using Rapid Learning Cycles and convergence, they will already be comfortable running smaller experiments and building subsystem prototypes to accelerate learning — cutting these large batches into smaller pieces.

Yet at some point, the first full system prototype needs to be built, and the first production proto needs to be run. If the group has done its work with emulators, simulators, small subsystem prototypes, convergence and other experiments, the team will be able to deliver a full system prototype that needs less work before moving on to the next phase.

The Physical Project Plan in Middle to Late Development

A physical product development team follows a logical sequence to complete the activities and produce the deliverables they need to hand off their product to production. In traditional product development, the Project Manager organizes this work into a GANTT chart that visualizes the dependencies between the activities so that the team can optimize the flow.

We believe that this visualization becomes even more important in late development. Figure 4.7 shows that teams transition from learning cycles to GANTT charts over middle development.

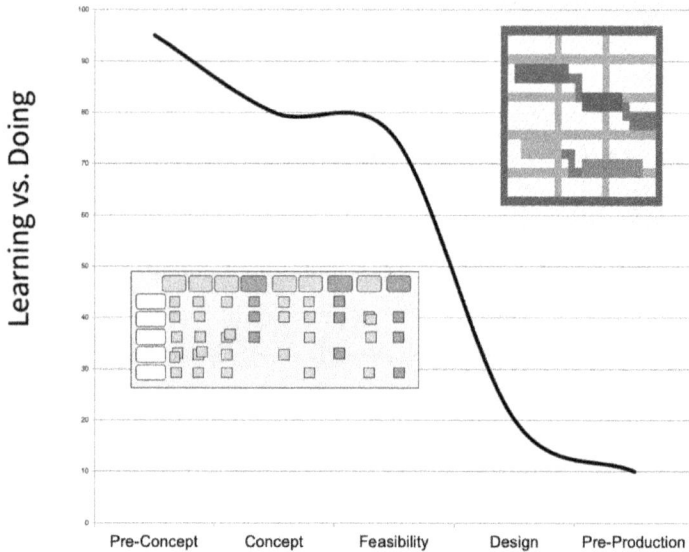

Figure 4.7: The Transition from Learning Cycles to GANTT Charts

A GANTT chart is not a plan — it's a model of a plan. Teams following a traditional process take this model too far. They try to make a detailed plan that covers an entire phase of work, and sometimes even the entire project. They believe that by making this plan they will get a good estimate of how long it will take to finish the project and get the product into production. But this is almost never true.

Traditional Plans Set Up a Team to Be Late
Engineering work is knowledge work, and knowledge work expands to fill the available time. This is why so few engineering deliverables get produced early. It's much more likely that a deliverable will be late because it

will take more time than the task was allocated. If everything has been planned out in detail, and nothing is early but a few things are late, then the entire project will be late — or people will have to work heroic hours at the end to keep it on time.

Project Managers can add buffers, but those quickly get consumed or eliminated in the name of efficiency. Team members can give generous estimates for the time it will take to do things, but then we run into the "knowledge work expands to fill the available time" problem.

To make things worse, long, detailed plans lead to a lower sense of urgency when things are late. If a team slips three days on a six-month plan, it doesn't seem like a big deal. Some groups get into games of "schedule chicken," competing to avoid being the first to admit that they will be late and hoping to get more time to finish without having to admit that they're late.

We can use a different approach to prevent this without losing the value of the overall plan that visualizes dependencies. When a team slips three days on a four-week plan, everyone can see it. Instead of making the entire project plan in one large batch, we can build multilevel plans with execution cycles, use real-time planning to reduce the batch size for each plan, and give the team fast feedback on how well their estimates reflect reality.

Multilevel Plans Visualize Flow

In Chapter One, we shared how multilevel plans helped pull together the pieces of the Rapid Learning Cycles framework. These plans provide increasing levels of resolution over shorter timeframes. We can use the same ideas in the Execution phases (which is what van Egmond did originally without using the term), as shown in Figure 4.8.

- Level 0 covers the entire project from idea to launch and has only the most important milestones: Gates and the target launch date. Changes here usually require leadership decisions.
- Level 1 covers the current phase of work, with major milestones, deliverables and any remaining Key Decisions. This is the level where the plan models key dependencies. In Early Development,

Level 0: Phase Gate Process

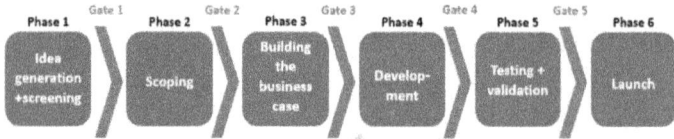

One Phase
or 6 Months

Level 1:
Major Milestones
and Deliverables

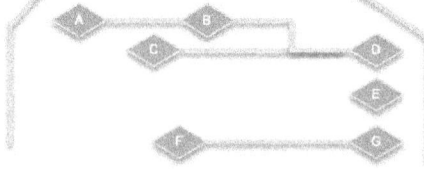

Level 2:
Execution
Cycle Plan with
Knowledge Gaps
and Deliverables

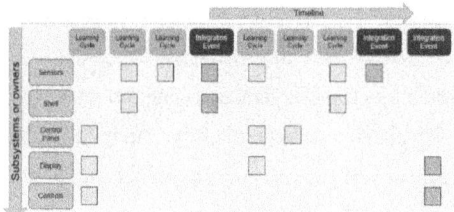

One
Execution
Cycle

Level 3:
Activity Plan

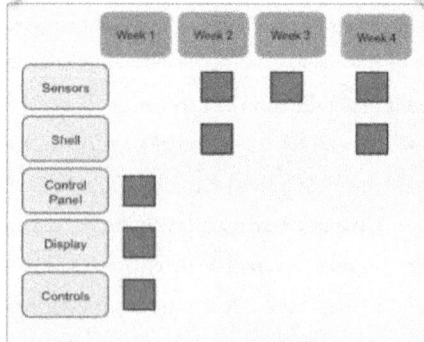

Figure 4.8: Multilevel Plans for Middle to Late Development

- it's focused on Key Decisions with a few other deliverables. In middle to late development, this is where major deliverables and milestones go. Teams need to see this dependency chain in order to make sure they are on target with their detailed plans. The GANTT chart for the project through launch lives at this level and is not broken down into more detail.

- Level 2 zooms in for a meaningful set of execution cycles, typically no more than 3-6 months. This is where the team puts the smaller deliverables that feed into the major deliverables, modeling the dependencies that are most helpful. But this plan will change often, so it's not useful to try to model them all.

- Level 3 is the detailed activity plan. We don't recommend that you create this at the team level. Instead, assign ownership for deliverables at Levels 1 and 2 and then let individuals manage their own work to get there. The Project Leader has more important things to do than model activities at this level. New team members who need help with this should get it from mentors or coaches.

Teams update these plans at the end of an execution cycle so that they always reflect the team's current understanding without the churn of constant updates. A good Project Leader will focus management attention on the Level 0 and Level 1 plans so that the team can optimize Level 2 and Level 2 without management interference.

What Goes into the Execution Cycles Plan?

Early attempts at Agile for hardware and SAFe® for Hardware have tried to answer this question by thinking like software developers. In that world, it makes sense to attempt to deliver a meaningful chunk of functionality that can be demoed at the end of a cycle. Hardware teams have tried to fit themselves into this model, but it just doesn't work well. You can't build up a golf cart the way you build up an app.

When we talk about meaningful bundles of deliverables, we mean the set of things that a team would ordinarily do if they had a traditional

GANTT chart guiding them, except organized into execution cycles to introduce cadence and fast feedback. The team will do the work itself in the order that makes the most sense — probably driven by lead times for prototype parts or tooling. Completed deliverables will be reviewed and approved at the end of an execution cycle.

As with Knowledge Gaps, some deliverables may take more than one execution cycle to complete, and this is OK as long as it doesn't make sense to break the deliverable down further. Within the execution cycle, teams can use a simple kanban board to track their progress on the deliverables, to see which ones are waiting, which ones may be stuck, and which ones just need a review to be completed.

We map these deliverables out into an Execution Cycle Plan to show when deliverables will be done so that the major deliverables and milestones will be reached on time. The time-based plan helps ensure that teams can see far enough ahead to know when deliverables with long lead times need to be started but not so far ahead that the team loses visibility.

Rolling Wave Planning Keeps the Team Focused

The early phases of a typical product development program are short enough that the team can map out a Learning Cycles Plan that covers an entire phase. But we learned early in this journey that some teams working in pharma, aerospace or other industries had very long development cycles, even for early phases. For them, there was not much value in planning learning cycles out more than six months. The teams would learn so much that the plan would be entirely different by then.

Instead, we introduced rolling wave planning, in which teams have high-level plans (Levels 0 and 1) that cover the entire phase but only planned out learning cycles (Level 3) for six months. Then at regular intervals, they would extend their Learning Cycles Plan for another few months. As these teams moved in the Execution phases, they just kept rolling the plan, adding in more deliverables as there were fewer Knowledge Gaps to close.

Some teams added a new learning cycle to the plan at the end of every learning cycle, but most found it better to do a bigger reset of the plan on less frequent intervals. A common pattern is to plan out six months for the first plan, then roll the plan every three months by adding three more months to the plan. At some point, usually after the gate between Feasibility and Detailed Design, it makes sense to start calling them execution cycles.

When deciding how many cycles to plan, teams need to balance two things: how much the plan is changing and how far ahead they need to see to accommodate deliverables with long lead times. Most teams can't really see more than six months in advance and don't really need to see that far ahead at the level of learning cycles, since they can track dependencies for the full program with Level 1 plans. At the same time, it doesn't make sense to plan only one learning cycle at a time because doing so hides critical information about when deliverables need to be done.

When teams manage their plans like this, and review the plan at all levels at every Learning Cycle Event, they maintain the long-term perspective they need on the overall plan while still visualizing the flow of work to be done to get them to the next phase. And they don't waste time reworking plans that are too detailed too early to be meaningful.

As they learn what it's actually going to take to deliver, they respond with flexible plans that can accommodate new information and adapt to changes. The plan itself has much less risk because it accurately reflects the current state of the team's knowledge about schedules and deliverables.

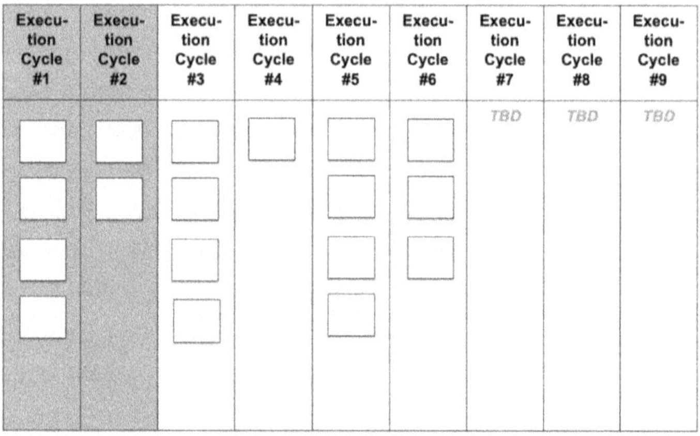

Execu- tion Cycle #1	Execu- tion Cycle #2	Execu- tion Cycle #3	Execu- tion Cycle #4	Execu- tion Cycle #5	Execu- tion Cycle #6	Execu- tion Cycle #7	Execu- tion Cycle #8	Execu- tion Cycle #9
☐	☐	☐	☐	☐	☐	TBD	TBD	TBD
☐	☐	☐		☐	☐			
☐		☐		☐				
☐		☐		☐				

Figure 4.9: Rolling Wave Planning After Execution Cycle #2

To Be More Agile, Eliminate More Risk

Physical product teams sustain the ability to be fast, flexible and responsive by eliminating risk. All of the tools we've described in this chapter work to remove risk by shortening the time between making a decision, executing the decision and validating the decision. When product teams eliminate these risks, they are much less likely to encounter a problem that requires long, slow loopbacks. When new information comes in, they will know where they still have flexibility to adapt and what the cost of change will be.

Convergence does this by delaying decisions. Emulators, simulators, subsystem prototypes, design reviews and other analysis tools provide rapid feedback without the expense and time of a full system prototype. Rolling wave planning provides rapid feedback on the team's ability to estimate, eliminates the waste of over-planning and reduces the risk of working to the wrong plan by helping the team stay focused on the overall goal without losing sight of the details.

Execu-tion Cycle #1	Execu-tion Cycle #2	Execu-tion Cycle #3	Execu-tion Cycle #4	Execu-tion Cycle #5	Execu-tion Cycle #6	Execu-tion Cycle #7	Execu-tion Cycle #8	Execu-tion Cycle #9
							TBD	TBD

Figure 4.10: Rolling Wave Planning After Execution Cycle #3

All of this makes it much more likely that the team will arrive at its first full system prototype ready for the transition to production, and ready for integration with firmware, cloud services and apps. In the next two chapters, we'll describe how to be fast, flexible and responsive as the final product and production process come together.

Slice-Based Integration to Build the Full System

Whe Katherine brought Kathy in to help with the Advanced Research team we described in Chapter One, she knew that Kathy had already been using these ideas in her own work for the later stages of product development. As a Senior Quality Engineer in HP's printer divisions, Kathy had extensive experience working with products that were bundles of hardware, firmware and software (drivers). She even worked with some early cloud applications (e-services). All of these products required significant integration effort in late development.

Typical Integration Testing Across Hardware, Firmware and Software

Kathy has witnessed firsthand the effects of the way most hardware/software products get tested. The major constraint in the process is the number of hardware prototypes available to test. These prototypes are expensive, and so tests tend to get organized around the need to maximize flow through those prototypes.

These tests tend to be organized around things like security or reliability with feature testing scattered across the test suites. The development teams have no way to know when any particular feature would be tested.

When Kathy began her research into new ways to think about this problem, she observed that integration testing started very late, perhaps three months before the end of the project. Once integration testing started, the development teams would get defects to fix. There were two problems with this scenario. First, weeks or even months had passed since the defects had been introduced, making them hard to find and fix. Second, the teams using Agile Software Development defined "done" as delivery into integration testing, but they weren't really done. They still had to fix the defects that would be found by integration testing before they could finish. This meant that their "done" wasn't predicting the final release date accurately.

Hardware Integration Causes Long, Slow Loopbacks in Software, Too

As we mentioned in the Chapter Four, product development teams with these types of products often integrate hardware and software in one very large batch, which creates long, slow loopbacks. We can improve the flow of work by making the batches smaller. Figure 5.1 shows how smaller batches provide faster feedback that can reduce the loopbacks substantially.

This is particularly true for products that contain both hardware and firmware (sometimes referred to as embedded software). Even when the firmware team uses Agile methods internally, the need to integrate with hardware can trigger long, slow loopbacks. The defects that are the source of these loopbacks are hidden from the team until they start putting the system together. That's because in middle development the teams work more or less independently.

Hardware Teams			
Proof of Concept	Detailed Design	Lab Proto	Production Proto

Test Set A | Test Set B

Long, Slow Loopbacks

Long reliability test

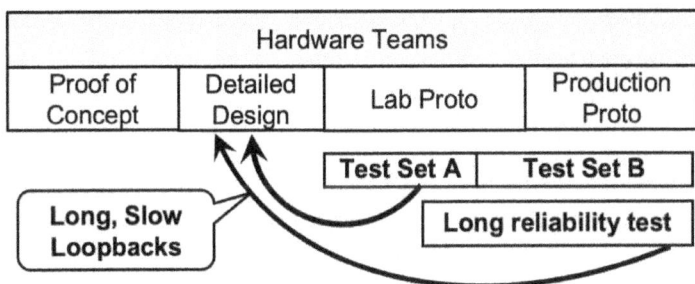

Figure 5.1: Long, Slow Loopbacks in Hardware Development

As we described in the previous chapter, the firmware team writes stubs to take the place of actual hardware or uses older versions of the product or breadboard emulators to test their work. They can do all of this using Agile methods to give them fast feedback, running tests and demos with whatever equipment they have. Figure 5.2 shows how this approach leads to short, fast loopbacks.

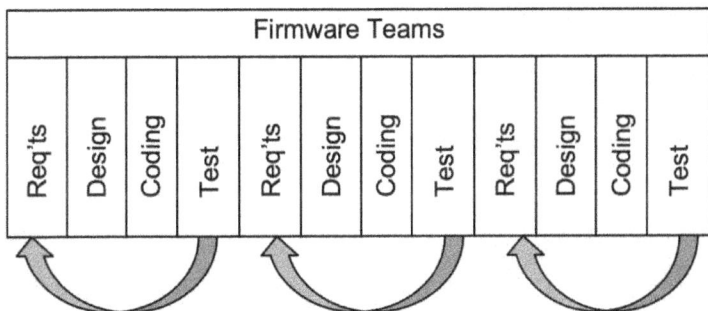

Firmware Teams											
Req'ts	Design	Coding	Test	Req'ts	Design	Coding	Test	Req'ts	Design	Coding	Test

Figure 5.2: Firmware Development Using Agile Software Development Has Short, Fast Loopbacks

But that only works to the extent that the test equipment or stubs accurately represent the final product. If the hardware team changes the design in some way that impacts the firmware, such as changing a sensor, the firmware team may have no way to test that. They may not even know the change occurred until the full system prototype shows up.

Once the product team has a full system prototype, they start running tests to validate the overall system. This is the work of a specialist team that designs and runs these types of tests. That function goes by a number of different names (Quality, Validation, System Test), but we will call them the Integration Test group.

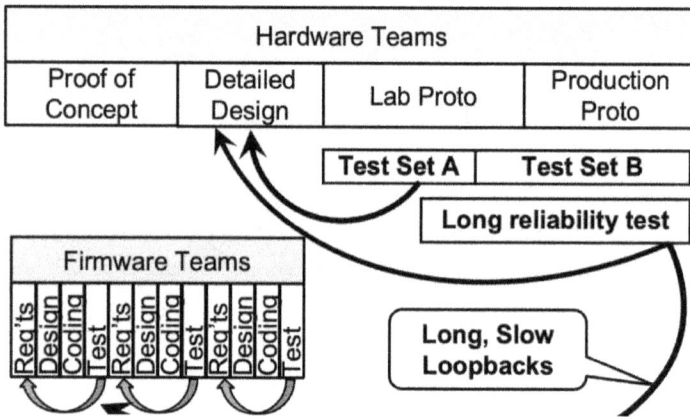

Figure 5.3: Hardware-Style Integration Causes Long, Slow Loopbacks for Firmware Teams

Integration Test usually organizes the tests into long test suites that minimize the number of expensive prototypes needed. But as shown in Figure 5.3, this practice only delays feedback to all the teams, making the long, slow loopbacks even longer. A firmware team may find it has to revisit code written weeks or months earlier. In worst case scenarios, the results of the tests are not yet available when it's time to build the next prototype, making loopbacks longer still.

Long Loopbacks Lead to Messy Integration

The problems uncovered in integration testing often aren't reported or even seen until the end of a long test suite. The problems uncovered here often require fixes that loop back to Detailed Design in both hardware and firmware. This is true even if the firmware team is using Agile, as shown in Figure 5.4. In fact, teams running Agile can deliver new firmware more frequently to Integration Test than Integration Test can handle.

Since firmware usually has more inherent flexibility at this point, Hardware will often ask if a problem with the mechanical design can be addressed with a firmware fix rather than an expensive change to the hardware in pre-production. This only adds to the burden for firmware teams — they don't have time or resources budgeted for these fixes. Meanwhile, the pressure is on for everyone to fix problems as fast as possible, especially if a problem is blocking other tests.

The larger the system, the more complicated this gets. Today, many products not only have hardware and firmware. They also have connectivity to cloud software services and apps. If teams try to handle these products the way they've handled simpler ones, Integration Test receives a barrage of new deliveries from all of these subsystem groups, none coordinated with each other because they are all trying to deliver fixes and late functionality as fast as possible.

Hard Design Freezes Make Things Worse

A Design Freeze is a theoretical moment in time when the design for a new product is frozen. It's theoretical because there are always changes after this milestone. But senior leadership in product development for physical products often assumes that all planned functionality will be delivered prior to the start of integration testing — and sometimes earlier than that.

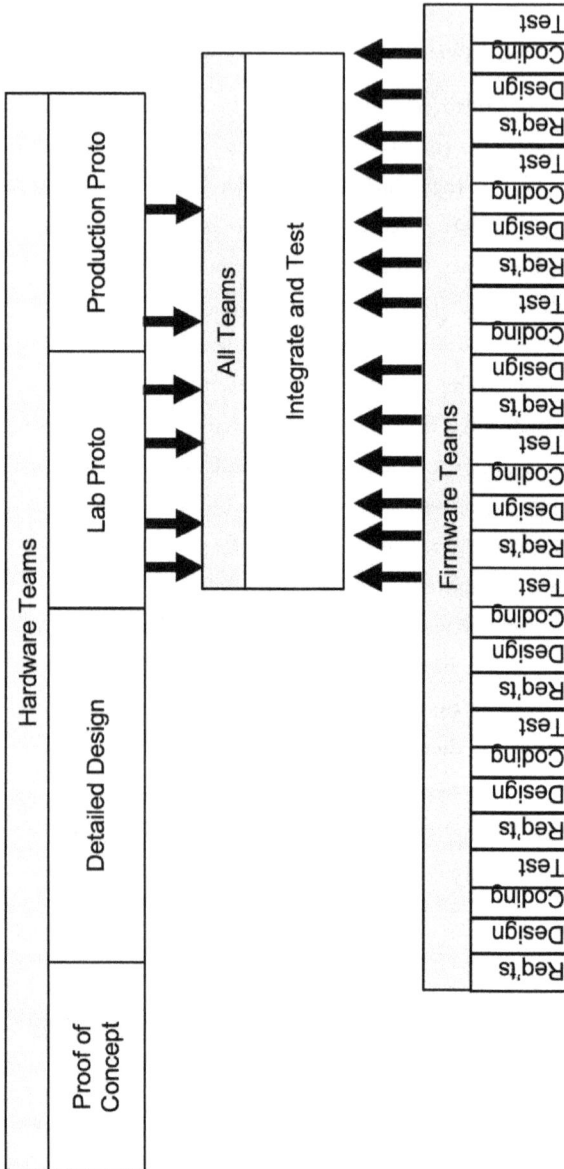

Figure 5.4: Hardware and Firmware Teams Deliver into Integration Testing

Without Coordination

The assumption isn't exactly true for even a purely physical product but it doesn't work at all if a product requires firmware, because firmware can — and still needs to — change. Sometimes, early user feedback or changing market needs leads to opportunities to improve the product with firmware changes only. If the changes truly reside only in firmware, such as a better UI design for a touchscreen, the cost and risk of change is low, and it makes sense to make the change.

Sometimes, the firmware is controlling parts of the system that are substantially different in production than they were even in full system builds with prototype parts. Such firmware must be "tuned" to the behavior of the final production hardware to deliver desired performance. Small changes in weight, balance, thermal expansion or other variables may change the values that firmware sends to pumps, motors, heaters or the user interface. In Chapter Six, we'll provide a way to incorporate this emergent behavior into integration testing.

Yet many organizations operate as if no new information will come in after Design Freeze. They assume that the production prototype will behave exactly the same way as the first system prototype builds. When this assumption proves false, the standard process has no way to accommodate the changes required. The firmware teams bear the brunt of this as they scramble to complete a lot of unplanned work.

Product teams in a typical organization experience all these pressures at once. Figure 5.5 shows what happens next. Software deliveries or "drops" are not aligned with prototype builds. Hardware teams are stuck in build-test-fix cycles of their own, and hardware becomes a moving target. It's easy to lose track of what needs to be done in order to deliver the working product on time. The teams are set up to experience project delays, cost overruns or other disappointing results from some very long, slow loopbacks.

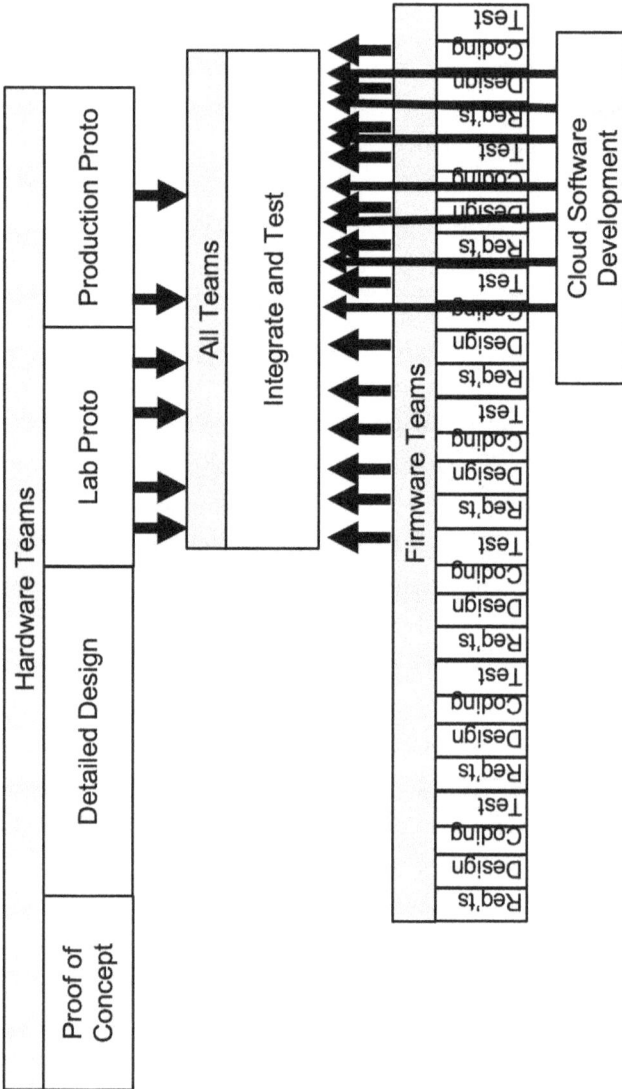

Figure 5.5: Unclear Relationships Between Software Drops, Hardware Drops and Integration Tests

Small Batches and Fast, Flexible Flow Eliminate Loopbacks

In 2009, Kathy's manager assigned her to lead a team to find a better way. He knew it could be done because he'd been part of a team that had succeeded in reducing these problems for a different HP division with similar issues. He tasked Kathy and her colleagues with finding out how to make the integration flow faster, predict the end date more accurately, coordinate all the teams more effectively and reduce those loopbacks. He shared his experience and pointed the team toward queueing theory to find the answers.

The fundamental problem with system integration is the mismatch between the large batches in integration testing and the small batches used by the firmware and software development teams. A full system prototype is itself a large batch. Integration Test exacerbated this by running long test suites. Meanwhile firmware and software teams were delivering their software in smaller pieces much more often.

Kathy found that when her team split integration work into smaller, more focused batches they were able to align the firmware and software drops, hardware changes and testing. Hardware didn't change as often as firmware, but the system could accommodate that if the hardware was delivered on a predictable schedule and the integration test suites were shorter.

If part of the team is familiar with Agile Software Development, they may be able to start by defining smaller batches right away because they are already used to working within a cadence. Others will need to split the schedule into evenly-spaced timeboxes of a few weeks' length that are on a regular cadence.

These timeboxes provide a structure to drive teams towards doing that integration in smaller batches. For each timebox, the teams will specify a set of tests that address a specific set of features. These test suites will be smaller than the traditional suites, and they'll be firmly linked to a known set of features. Just as with execution cycles in the last chapter, the timeboxes have no meaning on their own — they are just an arbitrary way to break down the integration plan. Figure 5.6 shows how this works.

When teams break down integration in this way, they get four benefits right away:

1. For any given timebox, all teams understand what does and doesn't need to be delivered in order to run the planned tests for this timebox.

2. Test teams understand whether or not those items have been delivered — which tells the program whether or not the system is ready to run (and pass!) a given test suite.

3. Teams get faster feedback because their new deliveries get tested right away, with shorter time intervals between finishing the work and receiving test results.

4. Teams can more easily see what's been done, and what still needs to be done.

Throughout this book, we've seen the value of a regular cadence to provide some structure and predictability in a system that is highly uncertain. Learning cycles, execution cycles and software sprints can all be coordinated on the same schedule or on nested cadences. The length of the integration timebox is the shortest of these cycles.

Now we need test suites and feature sets that fit into these timeboxes.

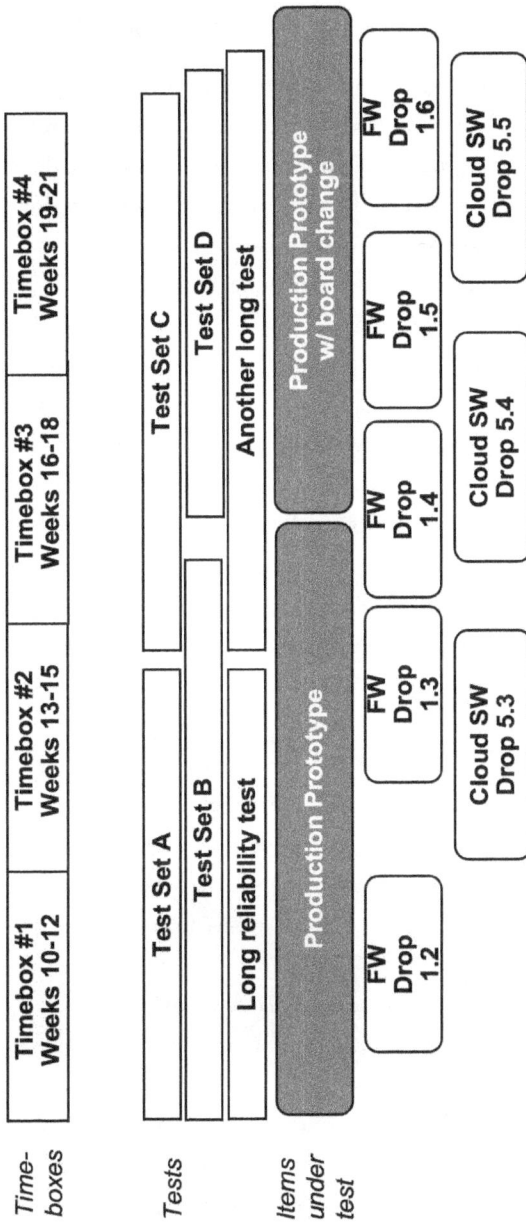

Figure 5.6: Integration Timeboxes Create a Cadence for Planning

Slice Through the Architecture

As we said in Chapter Two, an ideal batch is reasonably sized, delivers value and can be aligned with the ongoing development work across all subsystems and engineering disciplines. For integration, the ideal batch needs to pull together all the hardware changes, software drops, and test suites into a single set of testable behavior.

Kathy eventually started calling these batches "slices." A slice is a set of features or behaviors that will be tested in a single integration timebox. Each slice is an identified, testable set of functionality that requires contributions from multiple disciplines and subsystems. Each batch of functionality slices through the architecture just like slicing through a layer cake. This metaphor originated in software development, probably in an article by Bill Wake in 2003, and it's widely used in Agile Software Development.

The slices provide solid targets for the different engineering disciplines and the Integration Test group. Figure 5.7 shows that they all aim for the same target at the same time.

The slice is a lot larger than a typical user story — it's more the size of an epic or even bigger. A slice-based integration plan uses rolling wave planning to organize these slices in a logical sequence. The focus on a slice encourages teams to coordinate better across disciplines and define shorter tests that deliver feedback more quickly. Kathy and her teams found that this improved the flow of work and eventually the quality of the overall design.

Figure 5.8 shows some possible slices for an inkjet printer:

- Slice #1: Printer can print a test page in response to a button press.
- Slice #2: Printer can print a page sent from a connected PC.
- Slice #3: Printer can print a page sent from a mobile app.
- Slice #4: Printer can remind user to purchase more ink.

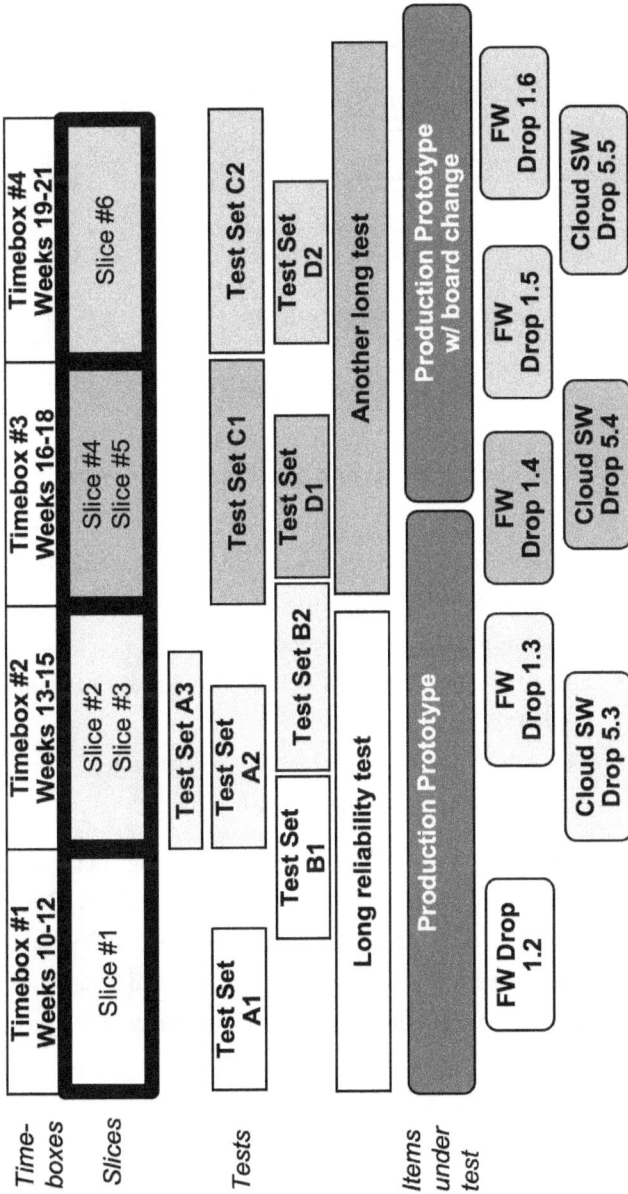

Figure 5.7: Integration by Slice Coordinates Prototypes, Drops and Tests

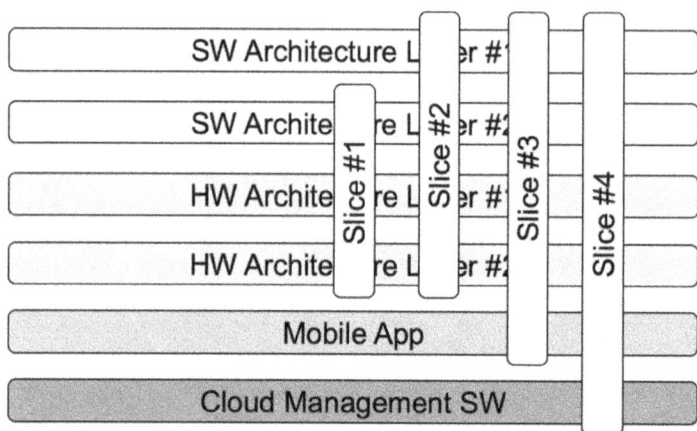

Figure 5.8: Slices Through the Architecture of an Inkjet Printer

These slices describe a set of high-level, end-to-end behaviors from the end user's perspective. There may also be slices describing behavior that will be used in the manufacturing process:

- Slice #19: Printer can run the production test that verifies alignment of the cartridge.
- Slice #20: Printer can perform post-production tests that verify that most recent firmware has been loaded.

This does not mean, however, that the product is being built incrementally on the hardware side! Even for Slice #1, the bulk of the printer needs to be designed and built. At this point in the project, the firmware and other software teams are building up the code they need iteratively while the hardware teams are mainly focused on fixing integration issues and getting the product into production.

Slices are effective only when all teams understand what each slice means and can relate it to their own work and to integration testing. This is one reason for defining a slice based on externally visible behavior: Teams need a common language for coordination, and the user's language is the one most shared across teams. "Confirm torque required to produce adequate sealing for the R3448 Pressure Valve using the W2394 washer" or "Implement Corvallis classes" don't tell the other teams what they need to do to support this slice.

It's also easier to assess progress when each slice delivers behavior that is meaningful for the end user. Even slices that refer to the architecture, such as "Printer functions normally with Rev 4.2 boards" still states the goal from the perspective of the end user.

Once Kathy and her teams had rough definitions of slices, they were ready to identify the deliverables that each discipline would need to contribute to each slice, and the integration tests that would be run on the slice. In this book, we're calling these subsystem deliveries "drops" instead of releases. A release is a complete batch that can deliver value for the organization, so a drop is not a release until it has passed all its tests.

A released integration slice delivers value to the organization. It's possible to demo the slice for feedback from others in the company. It may even be shared with Alpha or Beta Test customers for feedback from real users. Project Leadership can safely assume that the functionality is complete. While an integration slice is not exactly the same as a software epic, a series of released slices provides the same confidence in the plan as a series of released epics.

Kathy and her team found that splitting the integration work into slices made it much easier to coordinate the functionality delivered in each slice across disciplines. The integration batches were smaller, which created faster feedback and reduced those long, slow loopbacks.

How to Build a Slice-Based Integration Plan

When we've used a similar method at other organizations, we've found it can be awkward to move from a traditional hardware-centric integration plan to a slice-based integration plan, especially if the project is already past middle development, and the Integration Test Plan is based on a previous product. It's rarely practical to re-plan all the integration testing from scratch. Here's a way to start from where you are.

The Anatomy of a Slice-Based Integration Plan

In order to build a slice-based integration plan, you'll first identify four elements within your system (see Figure 5.9).

1. Timeboxes: The weeks remaining in development, organized into evenly sized boxes, typically two to four weeks long. If possible, align these with a firmware team's sprints or iterations so that the team drops new firmware into production at the start of each timebox. If you have another software team running shorter cadences, use that cadence instead. Small batches are better!

2. Items Under Test: The deliverables that are in testing during a timebox, including hardware prototypes or prototype variants, firmware drops and other software drops. Not every subsystem will drop a new item at the start of every timebox. Hardware prototypes, in particular, will often be used for several timeboxes before they are replaced with new versions.

3. **Slices:** The *features and behaviors* to be delivered in this timebox. The items under test have come together to deliver these features.

4. Tests: The specific tests planned for this timebox that will exercise the delivered features.

Timeboxes	Weeks 10-12 Mar 08-Mar 28	Weeks 13-15 Mar 29-Apr 18	Weeks 16-18 Apr 19-May 09	Weeks 19-21 May 10-May 30
Proto Build:	Prototype 1		Prototype 2	
Hardware Deltas:	<none>	GRS board 4.2	Initial packaging	TBD – board 4.3 release?
Firmware:	Drop 0.2 4/02	Drop 0.3 4/22	Drop 0.4 - TBD	TBD
Mobile SW:	<none>	<none>	Release 1.13 4/20	Release 1.14
Slice Definitions:	Print test page	Print from PC Rev 4.2 boards integrated	Print from mobile app Edge-to-edge photo printing	Mfg alignment test works Purchase more ink reminder
Tests Planned:	Basic functionality UX button response Life test	Print, all OS Board regression Life test, cont.	End-to-end mobile printing In-box durability	Mfg verification of cartridge alignment Low on ink Deplete ink

Figure 5.9: Anatomy of a Slice-Based Integration Plan

How to Build Your First Plan

Here is the step-by-step process to follow when first identifying the elements and building the plan.

1. Define the timeboxes.

2. Place the known plans for hardware prototypes into the "Proto Build" row.

3. Add in planned firmware and cloud software drops, using your usual naming conventions. At this point, some of the drops will have content and others may not yet be planned. This is OK.

4. Define slices that capture end-to-end testable behavior. You might find ideas in your firmware plans or in the Integration Test Plan or a combination of the two. No matter where slice definitions come from, they must be clear enough that every team from every discipline knows which deliverables they need to provide for which slice.

   The teams are likely to know a lot about what will be in the first few slices, and it will get increasingly fuzzy after that. This is normal. When you run out of information, leave the slices blank.

5. Put the integration tests on your plan, and try to capture the functionality each one assumes.

Now start iterating by comparing the slices with the planned integration tests.

Find the Slices

It might seem sensible to use requirements or specifications to define slices, but in practice we haven't seen this work well. Requirements and specifications often aren't organized into user-visible features and aren't listed in the order that they will be fulfilled. The system requirements may not even be in the requirements or specifications documents but instead embedded in the test cases.

Integration test suites often can't be easily chopped into tiny pieces, either. These test suites sometimes take a long time and for good reason—they run on expensive, scarce prototypes. Some run the same test multiple times to gather statistical data needed to assess reliability.

For these reasons, we suggest starting with the firmware and cloud software drops. Teams using Agile Software Development have already organized their work into small sets of discrete functionality known as user stories and epics. You may be able to use that list as-is. If you can't see end-to-end behavior in the epics, you may need to dig a little deeper or look at integration tests to find the right level for your slices.

Resolve Conflicts Between Test and Delivery

If the slices are delivered as shown, can the integration tests be run successfully? Sometimes the test plan will call for testing something that won't be ready until a later timebox. When it's obvious this will happen, the team has three options:

- Move the test later.
- Move feature development earlier.
- Split the test into smaller pieces so it only tests what's ready and then tests the rest later. This is often the best answer.

Keep working the plan until you have a schedule that looks feasible and accurately reflects the current state of your knowledge about the program.

Finalize the Plan

Try to finalize the plan with all the technical leads in the same room (at least virtually). Usually everyone needs to give a little bit. Some test suites will need to be broken into smaller test suites. Some long tests may have to span across more than one timebox. The contents of some software drops may need to be reorganized to fit with other disciplines and tests.

When you have a structure that aligns all of the disciplines with a clear set of targets at a manageable level of detail, you're done — with the first plan. The teams now have a shared view of the program's path towards full integration that accounts for cross-discipline dependencies. Once they have that view, they won't need a detailed GANTT chart showing all these dependencies in great detail. Instead, the technical leaders will use their slice-based integration plan to adapt to changing conditions.

Some of the work will be further ahead than the team can see, so the initial integration plan will have blank spaces and drops with no content, especially towards the end of the plan. That's OK because you will be updating the plan regularly.

Use Rolling Wave Planning to Update the Integration Plan

The previous chapter described real-time planning as a way to handle situations where teams couldn't see enough to build a good plan all the way to the end. The teams could, for example, decide to plan the next three timeboxes, and then add another timebox when the first one completes—always maintaining three timeboxes out from the end of the plan.

The slice-based plan gets updated at cross-discipline meetings, which also helps ensure that all teams are in regular communication, sharing new information as it comes up. These meetings should be frequent and short — as often as once per week. For teams, especially those new to this method, once per timebox is not quite often enough.

These meetings bring together the Technical Leads and Project Leaders from each of the involved disciplines, including the Integration Test group. Each discipline needs at least one person who can share progress updates and make decisions. The overall Project Leader usually runs the meeting, but the Chief Engineer or Chief Architect can also run it.

It works best when the first part of the meeting is run stand-up style, with each person sharing answers to three questions:

1. Has any item-under-test or planned testing changed?
2. Is anything in the way of getting ready for the next timebox?
3. What else do we need to know?

This encourages open sharing without going too deeply into details. After that, the team can move on to the rest of the agenda:

- Review the current timebox, and make adjustments as needed.
- Review the upcoming timebox, and make adjustments as needed.
- Fill in the next open timebox with a fully detailed plan.

The integration planning meetings focus more on the future than the present, so the team tries to avoid detailed discussions of defect lists and blocking issues. The only thing displayed is the integration plan. This is the meeting to discuss the issues that could block integration and testing next week, or in the next timebox.

It's also not a meeting to solve knotty technical problems, although the temptation to dive in will be strong. It's the place to raise such issues, but those that can't be solved immediately with just a comment or two should be taken offline.

This Is Not a Game of Perfect

There is no perfect integration plan. The primary benefit of a slice-based integration plan is the way it increases visibility and communication, especially around future blocking issues. Teams recognize when they need to update the plan. They can see where they are going and what they need to do, collectively, to get there.

You'll know you have a good plan when:

- Timeboxes are roughly equal to the size of software sprints/iterations.
- Slices are defined as delivering recognizable, testable functionality.
- Tests align well with the slices.
- The plan is visible and updated regularly, with all disciplines actively participating.
- Participants feel that the meetings are worth their time.

You'll know your plan's working when you can change it without much overhead or rework for any of the disciplines, including the Integration Test team. You waste less time fixing problems caused by miscommunication. People know what they need to deliver when, and what to do if their plans need to change. The loopbacks between development and test get shorter, and you may find ways to make them even shorter.

In most organizations, it's enough if the hardware, software and Integration Test teams work more collaboratively with less arguing. But you can go even further. In the next chapter, we'll describe a fully realized system for delivering earlier, smaller cycles that give feedback even faster.

CHAPTER SIX

The Integration Train for Large Organizations

The slice-based integration plan has demonstrated its value among the members of our community that have adopted it. But there's even more potential.

Many products today are connected to the Internet of Things (IoT), including some that have never had any need to talk to other devices before. They are bundles of hardware, firmware, connectivity, cloud services and apps. The integration challenges for these products are exponentially greater than they are for a simple mechanical product. This is especially true for the first IoT product, when the product team needs to build and validate the entire architecture, the user experience and the business value for connected products at the same time.

With such large, complex teams, the sheer number of players tends to overwhelm the simple slice-based planning method. In this chapter, we'll share the next evolution in this thinking: the Integration Train. This method is newer and less well-tested than the others we've described so far, but early results are promising.

Coordinated Delivery Across Multiple Subsystems, Disciplines and Groups

The Integration Train uses more tools from queueing theory — cadence, WIP control and prioritization — to coordinate delivery of the slices and minimize feedback loops. The method also improves the way the system is divided into slices in order to further reduce those long, slow feedback loops.

We used the same principles to build the slice-based integration plan but in a casual way that was suitable for products with a handful of groups involved. The Integration Train applies these principles with more rigor because the groups are larger, the margins of error are smaller and the communication needs are greater.

The Integration Train method is based on software release trains of the 1990s and early versions of SAFe®, but most people wouldn't call it a release train. Release trains actually release software to users — they coordinate things like the release of updates to the iOS App Store. Those releases deliver immediate user value in the form of less buggy, more functional apps. The Integration Train doesn't release the product — it coordinates the integration of the product as the hardware matures and the firmware builds towards being feature-complete. It's also considerably different from the Agile Release Train (ART) as seen in SAFe® today.

Cadence to Simplify Planning and Save Time

The Integration Train uses timeboxes just like the slice-based planning described in the previous chapter but with one significant difference: An Integration Train assumes that any given slice will enter Integration Test *on the first day of the timebox.* We give up some flexibility to gain more predictability.

If a large, complex team doesn't establish this rule, the different engineering disciplines will drop their latest version into integration testing on different days within a single timebox, and those days won't be the same from one timebox to the next. The team can't keep track of what is actually in Integration Test on any given day, and which tests should be run. Any benefit gained from increased flexibility is swallowed up by the overhead of managing the plan.

The term "Integration Train" describes the practice of all teams delivering into integration testing at the same time. The Integration Train operates on a regular, pre-determined and predictable schedule — and that makes all the difference with so many groups involved.

You can think of the slices as passengers and the deliverables as their luggage. If all the deliverables for a given slice aren't ready when it's time to go, then that slice misses the train and has to catch the next one.

That's because the deliverables on this train all go into integration testing together. Each slice that goes into integration testing must have all the deliverables it needs to pass the planned tests — and those deliverables should be ready for Integration Test. That means that the individual teams have already found and fixed all the issues they can find on their own.

The first integration test is often a smoke test that checks whether the assembled system is working well enough to continue with more rigorous tests. Then Integration Test continues with tests to confirm the behavior specified for the slice. This only works if everything needed for the slice is ready for this level of testing.

Figure 6.1 shows what an Integration Train Plan looks like. The plan shows the trains, the slice sets (the full plan would have actual slices in those sets), the test suites and the items under test. Firmware and cloud software drops coordinate with the start of the trains, and hardware prototypes cross multiple trains.

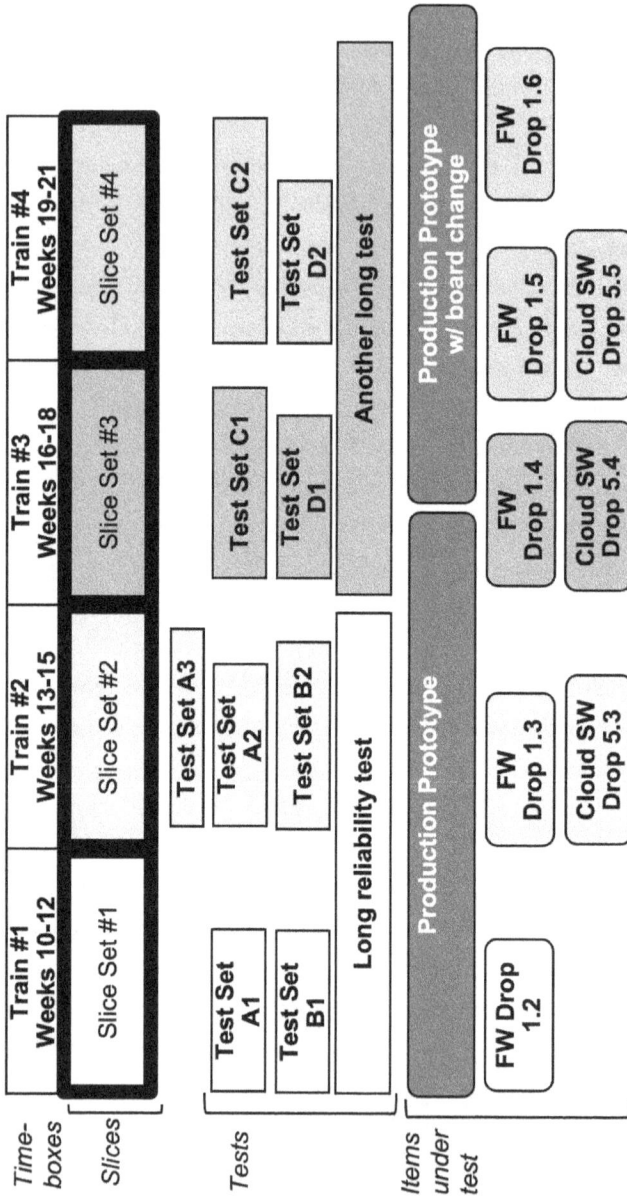

Figure 6.1: Integration Train Plan

Stick to the Train Schedule and Stay on the Tracks

When a slice isn't ready to enter integration testing on its targeted date, it misses the Integration Train. It will need to wait for the next train. Sometimes people assume this will cause delays, but this rule actually speeds up development overall for large, complicated projects by reducing the overhead of managing all the exceptions.

Integration testing is expensive and takes time. When a new slice boards the train, the test group may have to load software onto chips, set up prototype hardware, replace boards and configure equipment. If any of the deliverables are missing for a slice, and yet the slice continues, this work may have to be redone.

At a minimum, the Team Leaders will waste a lot of time talking about whether to hold off on integration, how long to wait for the missing deliverable, or how to figure out the impact on the Test team and all other teams. All this discussion leads to more meetings, more email, more coordination. It wastes a lot of time better spent producing those missing deliverables.

With an Integration Train, the organization only has one question to ask: "Is this slice ready to get on the train now?" If the answer is "No," then everybody knows exactly what will happen: The slice will move from this train to the next one, while the Integration Test group plans testing for the slices that actually made it on the current train.

This only works if the trains are not too far apart. Missing a train on a commuter line is not a big deal if the next one is in three minutes — but certainly is a big deal if the next one isn't until tomorrow. In our experience, two to four weeks is often enough.

At the same time, there are reasons to violate this rule that make sense, especially at first. When the team is getting close to a major milestone, it may not be practical to move slices from one train to the next. As teams gain experience with this method, they'll learn what it's like to have a fixed number of regular delivery dates into integration testing versus a larger number of constantly shifting dates.

They'll experience the reduction in overhead and increased clarity for themselves. That will give them strong motivation to uphold this rule and stay on the tracks. In the meantime, the discussions themselves will lead to better communication so that teams spend less time on planning and more time on engineering.

Accelerate the Train with Smaller, Earlier Batches

Every time a slice goes into integration testing, there is some overhead. It may seem like the best way to reduce this overhead is to deliver less often and run the tests in large batches. In Chapter Two, we showed that systems flow better when batches are smaller and more frequent. We can improve flow by making the test suites smaller and by making the slices smaller.

Smaller slices deliver value earlier. A slice delivers value by providing information about the quality and acceptability of the product *and* about the progress of the project. Smaller slices and more frequent Integration Trains deliver both kinds of value sooner. When teams know that they have *finished* features to an acceptable level of quality and usability, they can use that knowledge to measure progress with certainty.

All of this also speeds up feedback loops, making it easier to find the source of problems and prevent the compounding errors that arise when a problem is not caught early and becomes embedded deep into the system design.

All of these benefits far outweigh the drawback of extra overhead. When slices are smaller, and Integration Trains are more frequent, it's easier for teams to follow the rule — all needed deliverables must be ready for a slice to make the train — because there is less to deliver and the consequences of missing a train are less severe. We can accelerate even more by starting the Integration Train even earlier in development.

Build Early Slices to Accelerate Integration

Slices nearly always consist of working features because working features deliver the most information about the usefulness and quality of the planned features and about the progress of the project. However, the earliest slices may not be all that compelling from a user perspective. The earliest slices often resemble the "walking skeletons" that authors like Johanna Rothman describe as the earliest outcome of Agile Software Development.

Here are some possible early slices for an inkjet printer:

- Minimum capability from a user perspective: Can the system print at all?
- Minimum capability from an architectural perspective: Can the subsystems talk to each other reliably? Do they fit together? For systems controlling multiple objects in real-time, a team might demonstrate that the communications are in place and happening fast enough.

Again, these are primarily firmware- or software-focused slices. The hardware team's schedule is still driven mainly by lead times into production, and their first full system prototype should be able to handle these early slices. Later slices will gradually integrate more of the architecture as the physical parts continue to mature, so the behaviors become broader and more realistic.

Slices can also capture capabilities, such as reliability, in addition to features. This forces the team to discuss when the system will be mature enough to test a specific capability.

Characteristics of a Good Slice

Teams using the simple slice-based integration plan introduced in Chapter Five have room for error when it comes to defining slices. Because larger teams face complex integration challenges, they must define slices more precisely, satisfying these criteria for a well-defined slice:

- The name and definition of each slice captures the scope clearly.
- The team is aligned around what needs to be developed and which tests ought to pass when the slice is delivered.
- The slice is small enough to be tested within one timebox most of the time.
- The slice either delivers a usable set of behaviors or a capability that some user cares about, or it answers a question critical to further development.
- The slice is defined to allow the team to test riskier aspects of the system first — as soon as they have enough to start meaningful tests.

Slice A: Ink cartridges move across the page area to deliver ink.

This slice demonstrates that the hardware architecture is functional and that the first full system prototype is working well enough for integration to proceed.

Slice B: Printer can print a test page in response to a button press.

This slice demonstrates a larger (though still not end-to-end) flow of functionality across the architecture. It also marks the arrival of a key piece of testability. The ability to print a test page, although of little interest to end users, will be used extensively in later tests.

Slice C: Color registration is precise (the printer prints clearly in color).

In this slice, the printer should be capable of laying ink onto exactly the right spots on the paper to produce clear, crisp lines of accurate color.

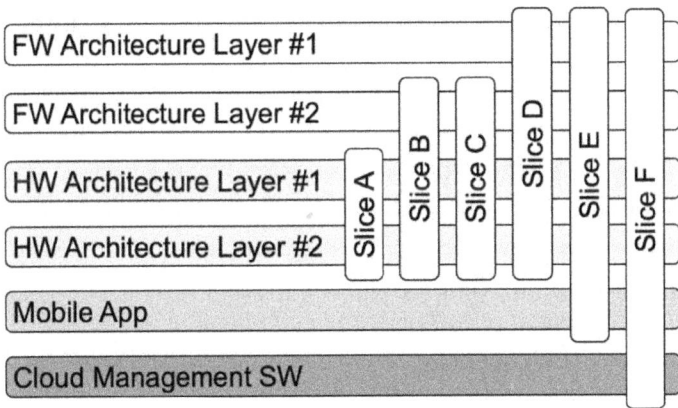

Figure 6.2: Some Slices Through an Inkjet Printer

Figure 6.2 shows some examples from a hypothetical inkjet printer.

Since inkjets produce tiny dots, this requires precise control of the hardware by the firmware, and testing it requires printing standard patterns to verify that the registration is correct. It's not exactly something a user would do, but it's necessary for almost anything a user wants to do with a color printer. This behavior is emergent — it cannot be finalized until the production hardware is available.

Slice D: User can print a page from a PC.
This is the first slice that's a legitimate end-to-end user scenario.

Slice E: User can print a job from a mobile app.
Completion of this slice could be a gate for starting beta testing with users.

Slice F: Printer can remind user to purchase more ink.
This is a typical end-to-end user scenario slice.

Emergent Behaviors Appear at Integration Points

In the above examples, Slice C (Color registration is precise) is a bit different than the others because it tests emergent behavior. This means that the behavior can only be approximated before the entire system is in place. If a product requires precise control of mechanical or electrical parts by firmware in real-time, chances are that some area of the product has emergent behavior. Figure 6.3 shows how this works.

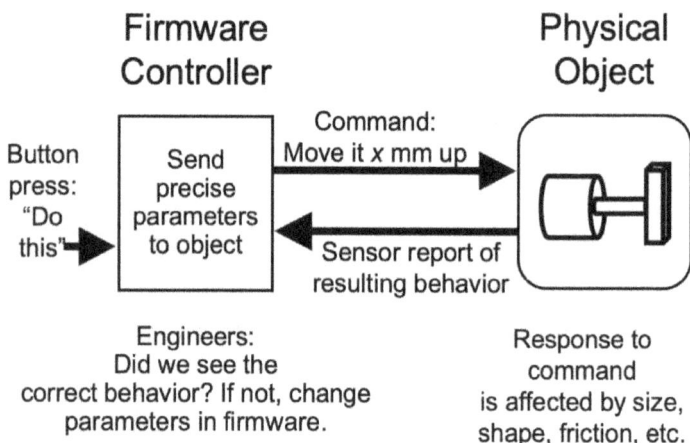

Figure 6.3: Emergent Behavior

In inkjet printers, color registration is a complex interaction involving the ink cartridge, motors, controllers and firmware that work together to control the movement of the paper and the firing of the cartridge nozzles. Prototype parts for both the printer and the ink cartridge are likely made using different manufacturing methods and often different materials. This means that even the last full system prototype built in the lab can be substantially different from the first production prototype. When they are different, this leads to subtle differences in how the system behaves when it's printing — different enough to throw off color registration.

Because printing must be so precise, these small differences mean that early tests with prototypes cannot accurately predict whether or not the final product will meet the specifications for accurate color registration.

Early tests can only assess whether or not there's a major problem that prevents the system from working at all, and whether or not the system responds in a predictable way to changes, such as parameter changes in the firmware configuration.

In our example, Slice C can only be finished once the team has production prototype printers and production cartridges. Only then can the values for key parameters be finalized to deliver accurate color registration. Good firmware teams will design their code so that they only need to update the parameters in order to dial in the right values quickly once the final hardware is available.

Teams have these types of slices anywhere they have complex interactions that cannot be accurately modeled by prototypes. They are often, but not always, interactions between hardware and software with algorithms that depend on the physical characteristics of the hardware. Any system involving precision control of small mechanical parts or fluid dynamics typically has considerable emergent behavior.

These physical characteristics can only be modelled in CAD and prototype parts — the nature of the production process itself changes these characteristics. This means that the final system must be tuned and then tested for such emergent behavior only with realistic, near-final hardware made from production tools.

This can be a source of conflict between hardware and firmware teams if the development process assumes that hardware and firmware will freeze at the same time, prior to the release to production.

Teams must allow time in the schedule for this tuning process, or they are setting themselves up for an unexpected delay. Slices help by making these behaviors and their consequences a lot more visible — and by identifying certain slices with emergent behavior.

How to Start the Integration Train by Working Backwards

In Chapter Five, we described how a team builds its first slice-based integration plan by working backwards. These first attempts to define slices require give-and-take between the multiple development plans and the Integration Test Plan. A cross-discipline team iterates on the plans from multiple directions until the contents of the deliveries and the tests line up. Teams do the same thing to build an Integration Train, mindful of the additional rigor.

Work Backwards to Find Slices — Then Slice Them Even Smaller

These first attempts at slice definitions often start by looking at the software deliveries and the integration tests that are already planned. Once the team has some experience, the technical leads will begin to see that some of the long test suites cause slow loopbacks. They'll work with Integration Test to split the test suites into shorter ones that make it easier to align the deliveries with the tests.

For example, a test suite might contain a whole set of end-to-end tests:

- Printer reminds user to buy ink.
- User prints glossy photographs.
- Printer runs out of paper.

These are all major tests that exercise numerous subsystems at once. When test suites are this large, many different deliverables have to be put into integration testing at once in order to start the test. It will be easier to manage the flow of work if the team splits up the test suite to group similar scenarios together.

Meanwhile, some tests for reliability and similar capabilities are inherently long because the same test needs to be repeated many times to get data that can be analyzed with statistics. These tests won't fit neatly into smaller slices and should be allowed to run across multiple timeboxes.

Early Slices Reduce Risk by Delivering Early Information

In Chapter Four, we described the importance of reducing risk in product development, and early Integration Trains should focus on risk reduction. Features that require coordination between multiple layers of hardware, software and services have more integration risk. Early slices can reduce this risk by delivering early information about the integration. This often means a slice that cuts across only part of the architecture, with other parts stubbed out or simulated.

Here is an imaginary example:

A team is working on a feature to remind the user to buy ink, then direct them to a place where they can purchase the ink online. On the hardware side, the printer needs to recognize when ink is getting low. The physical parts required have long lead times, so validating these early is important to make sure that the team is on track for production release.

The team defines an early slice called "Printer Displays Low Ink Message" specifically to validate that the hardware is recognizing low ink and sending an appropriate message to the firmware. It doesn't matter what the message says at this point. It could even be a pattern of flashing LEDs on the printer's breadboard. This provides the hardware team with the certainty they need to go into production with their long-lead-time parts.

Later on, the team will develop the user interface for the "Low Ink" message as displayed on the PC. The team defines a slice: "Printer Displays Low Ink Message on PC." It succeeds when the user sees a clear message on their PC when ink is low.

The online service to provide the ability to purchase replacement ink cartridges is delivered much later, as part of a slice "Remind User to Buy Ink." This slice could even be delivered after the printer has been released onto the market if it's included in a driver update.

Emergent Behavior Needs Multiple Slices

Emergent behavior in particular may need to be developed in several slices that are not usually located close to each other in the Integration Train plan:

1. Demonstrate that all programmer-configurable software options can be configured successfully (no physical prototype required).
2. Demonstrate that changing the configurable options changes the behavior of the moving parts in predictable ways that can be controlled (subsystem prototype or early full system prototype required).
3. Demonstrate that a specific configuration of these options results in the final desired behavior (production prototype required).

The first test requires only the software and an emulator or test harness and may be done by the software team alone before the Integration Trains get underway. The second slice needs early hardware that's representative enough to allow for predictable behavior. The final slice requires near-final hardware. But if the first and second slices are both successful, the third slice can move through fast.

The slice definition is a technical job and not one for Project Managers. Teams need a deep understanding of the technical dependencies — not just the schedule dependencies — between parts, between disciplines and between Engineering and Test. Without this technical cross-discipline work, it's far too easy to create a plan that looks good on paper but cannot be executed.

How to Start the Integration Train by Working Forwards

As teams gain experience, they can begin building in even more agility by working forwards from basic principles. When a team thinks from the beginning about the order in which to build things, they can identify more opportunities to plan the development and integration in small batches that deliver value.

Teams can start by brainstorming a list of technical questions to answer, starting with a series of "Does X feature work?" Another series of questions emerges around "Does the product meet specifications for X capability?" Then teams can blend the answers with an Integration Train plan adapted from a previous program to ensure they don't miss anything. As they build the plan, they can continue to look for opportunities to make smaller slices.

Towards a System for Agile Hardware Development

In the last four chapters, we looked at hardware development from idea through Feasibility, Detailed Design and System Integration. We identified batches and looked for ways to reduce batch sizes, put repeating events on a cadence and limit work-in-progress.

When a team uses Rapid Learning Cycles to make better decisions in Early Development, and when they group their deliverables into execution cycles in middle development, they are positioned to keep their Integration Train moving with few long, slow loopbacks.

They have become fast, flexible and responsive from idea to launch.

CHAPTER SEVEN

The Agile Development System for Physical Products

At the beginning of this book, we shared the experiments we've run to understand how to make the early stages of physical product development faster, more flexible and more responsive. In Chapter Two, we described the mechanism that led to repeatable results for the teams we've worked with us. The rest of the book described how we have used the same principles to develop practices and tools that fit physical product development from idea to launch.

Now, we put the pieces together. We'll call this overall system Agile for Physical Products because it helps physical product teams become faster, more flexible and more responsive — using the same principles that lie underneath Agile Software Development.

Agile Software Development Doesn't Work for Physical Products

We'll also use this term because some organizations have decided they want their entire businesses to be more agile — and interpret that to mean they need Agile Software Development practices and tools because there hasn't been a clear alternative. If you are making physical products in an environment like that, this system will give you a better alternative to direct adaptations of Scrum or SAFe®, such as SAFe® for Hardware or Modified Agile for Hardware.

These attempts to replicate the practices and tools designed for software development lead to known undesired side effects that we shared in earlier chapters: overwhelming backlogs that obscure the big picture, too much project management overhead and too much focus on Demos and doing a lot of stuff at the expense of learning. We've explained how we can predict these effects from the differences between the batches and queues in hardware development versus software development, and we've observed these effects with real physical product teams.

Worse, they don't solve the biggest problems that physical product teams actually have: long, slow loopbacks that arise from revisited decisions.

Agile for Physical Products Eliminates Long, Slow Loopbacks

Agile for Physical Products eliminates those loopbacks at their source and shortens the loopbacks that result from execution errors. We've shown that all the practices we've incorporated into this book have been tested on real physical product development teams, and we've shared how we tested and built up these ideas by collaborating with those teams to develop the practices and tools that would help these teams become faster, flexible and more responsive.

The Overarching Framework: Healthy Phase Gates

As we described in Chapter Four, almost all physical product organizations have phase-gate PDPs, which require teams to go through a Gate Review before entering the next phase. Healthy phase-gates focus the Gate Reviews on the investment decision to continue. If the team passes through a gate, the next phase will often require more resources and perhaps a different level of funding. In healthy phase-gate PDPs, these are business decisions.

Physical product teams that have unhealthy phase-gates or no phase-gates at all often have only loose business controls: either the product teams don't need management approval for much, or the senior leaders micro-manage because otherwise they'll lose control. On the one extreme, the Gate Review is a rubber stamp; on the other, it may as well be an audit. Neither extreme helps the senior leaders make the right business decision.

Teams trying out the practices in this book can function within an unhealthy phase-gate PDP, and a startup team working on a single first product may not need a phase-gate PDP. But Rapid Learning Cycles and the other practices will expose the problems in an unhealthy PDP. Teams will be able to see when deliverables are due too early for the team to have confidence in the decisions embedded in those deliverables. Leaders will be able to see which decisions feed into the Gate Review decision, and which ones can and should be reviewed elsewhere. Over time, the product groups that have collaborated with us the longest have shifted towards healthier phase-gate PDPs that focus on business decisions.

A startup can get its first product out without this structure, but a scale-up needs a phase-gate model as soon as the teams are juggling multiple products within a product family. That's the point in time when leaders have to choose from a lot of ideas to get down to a few prioritized development programs that require increasing levels of investment.

Katherine has seen over and over again that the Rapid Learning Cycles framework drives a team towards healthy phase-gate PDPs because it improves the quality of decision making. The team's sponsors and stakeholders are more engaged because they've been involved at Integration Events. The framework visualizes the flow of Key Decisions into deliverables and the Gate Review decision itself. The process of building a Learning Cycles Plan exposes questions about Last Responsible Moments that push final deliverables later.

Rapid Learning Cycles: The Leading Edge

The early stages of a phase-gate PDP are all about learning enough to decide whether or not to make the investment to learn more. The earliest phase often serves to screen: Is this idea worth investigating? Then a small team moves into concept development: Is it worth developing into a product? Then a larger team investigates feasibility: Can we develop this product so that it delivers sufficient customer and business value while meeting our thresholds for cost and quality?

This is the natural home for Rapid Learning Cycles because the framework keeps teams focused on answering questions and making decisions that set up the later stages for success: In which market will we launch first? Which partner will we choose to help us develop a key subsystem? Which material will we use for a major component of the system?

From an agile perspective, the goal of these early phases is to deliver a feasible concept that can be commercialized with as many risks eliminated as possible and others well-understood. The concept rests on a set of Key Decisions that have been made at the right time with the right people and with the best knowledge available. In Detailed Design, teams work to execute those decisions.

Execution Cycles: The Bridge from Feasibility to Full System Prototype

When the team gets to the Execution phases, they'll know that their detailed design work is resting on a foundation of good decisions made earlier in development. The work of the Detailed Design phase is the work of executing many decisions, most of which are well-known, standards-driven, low-impact or easy to change.

Figure 7.1 shows how Rapid Learning Cycles and execution cycles blend together in these middle stages of development. The "cycle" is the same. The batches within each cycle will transition from mostly Knowledge Gaps to mostly deliverables. As the team moves from early phases to later ones, the cycles will get longer — from perhaps two weeks in Concept Development to four or six weeks by the end of the Execution Phase.

Phase Gate Product Development Process

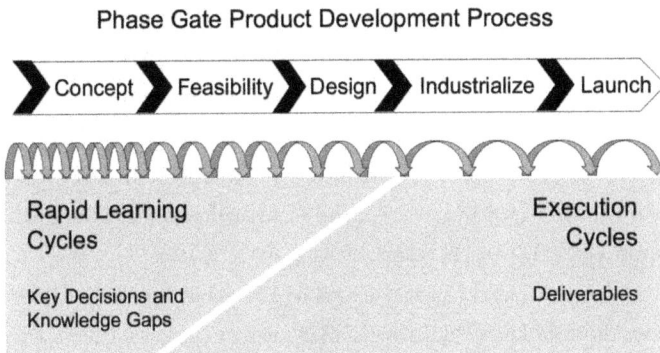

Figure 7.1: The Transition from Learning Cycles to Execution Cycles in Middle Development

As we described in Chapter Four, "deliverables" is a catch-all term for the requirements and specifications documents, CAD models, requests for proposal, purchase orders, finished drawings, test plans and other items needed to move a physical product from design to production.

Most of the decisions that are embedded in these deliverables can be made and executed early because they have lower risk, perhaps even a proven solution. All other things being equal, the team should focus on implementing those non-Key decisions first, and then turn their attention to the stuff in the riskier areas of the project as the Key Decisions arrive at their Last Responsible Moments.

While the hardware teams are doing detailed design, the firmware and possibly cloud software teams can use Agile methods to produce functional and reliable software using emulators, simulators, and early prototypes. Execution cycles and planning by slices help hardware and software work effectively together, providing support to each other's work, particularly around developing emergent behaviors.

Integration Slices and Integration Trains to Drive Towards Launch
If the team has done everything we've suggested, they will arrive at their first full system prototype with a product that is much more mature. It may have taken a little longer to get to this point, but the team has greater confidence in the decisions they've made up to this point. If their firmware and other software partners are using Agile methods, the entire product can move rapidly towards launch.

That isn't to say things will always be 100 percent smooth. There are always those "unknown unknowns" that creep in: feedback from early users who can finally experience the whole product, system-level defects not seen until the whole system is put together, vendors who overpromise and underdeliver.

To the extent that they've already found and fixed everything they can at a subsystem level, these will be the *only* problems they have. With fewer changes, the team should be able to work at a reasonable pace to get from here to launch.

Physical Product Teams Continue Execution Cycles to the End
Hardware teams will be occupied with the design and validation of tooling and the production process, finding fixes and workarounds to any problems that arise. They will deliver a series of increasingly mature prototypes, usually starting with prototypes built in their labs and ending with production units that are ready to be shipped.

Other types of physical products, such as chemicals or biologicals, may have different processes for upscaling, but the general pattern is the same: Prove out the product at lab scale, and then design and run industrial trials until they have a good product they can produce at scale. They still want to find every problem they can at lab scale before running industrial trials.

All of this work can be organized into execution cycles, which should be nested to fit the cycle time to turn around a new prototype build: If a prototype build takes eight weeks, then teams should run two- or four-week execution cycles (eight weeks is too long).

Firmware and Other Software Teams Use Agile

We've said many times that Agile Software Development solves the problems that software teams often encounter. Even in high-reliability and heavily regulated environments like medical products and aerospace, the principles of queueing theory still apply. In fact, some of the earliest applications of small-batch development were at NASA on Project Mercury. Even if the concept of a MVP has a much higher threshold, and the criteria for completion are much more rigorous, these teams still benefit from breaking down their work into smaller batches and validating those batches of work right away.

In fact, because of the emergent behaviors we described in Chapter Six, it's even more important that firmware teams know how to work effectively in short iteration cycles. They will be under a lot of time pressure to dial in the final firmware at the end, when the production prototypes are ready and the business is set to launch.

Integration Slices Coordinate Across Groups

The integration slice is the interface between the hardware groups running execution cycles and the software groups running Agile. It leverages the fact that all of these groups are running cycles, even if the cycle lengths are not the same because the batches are comprised of different things. It provides a standard way for teams to decide together what they will test and therefore which test suites will be run for any given slice.

Phase Gate Product Development Process

> Concept > Feasibility > Design > Industrialize > Launch >

Rapid Learning
Cycles

Execution
Cycles

Key Decisions and
Knowledge Gaps

Deliverables

| Prototype Builds | Final Product |

Integration Timeboxes | 1 | 2 | 3 | 4 | 5 | 6 | ... | n |

Software Drops

Agile Software
Development

User Stories

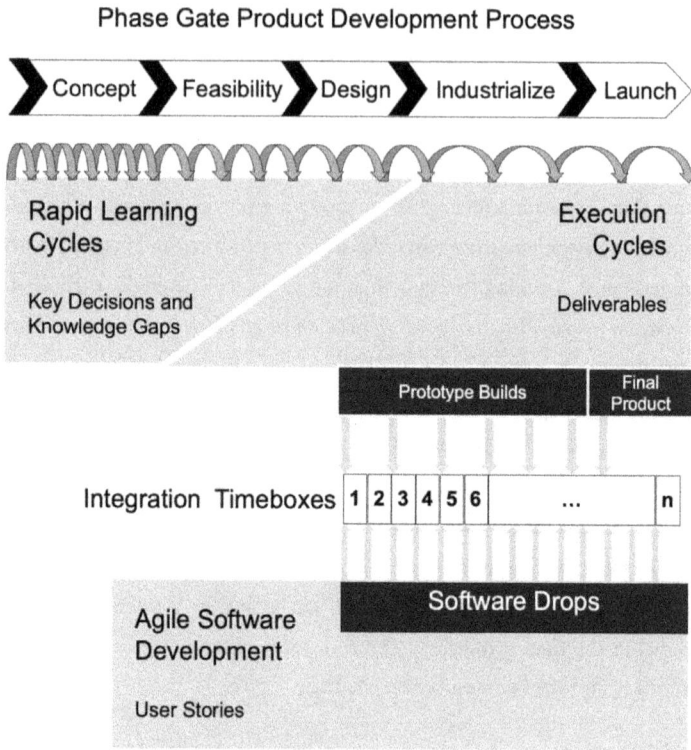

Figure 7.2: The Agile for Physical Products System for Products that Include Software

Figure 7.2 shows how integration timeboxes coordinate the prototype builds from the hardware teams with the drops from software teams. The hardware builds will evolve from subsystem prototypes to system prototypes to production prototypes and, finally, to finished products. The slices coordinate the software drops and integration testing with these builds.

There are two important things to note here. First, the prototypes from Hardware do not represent features or functionality that is "done" in the way that the software drops are "done." Until the final product has been put into production, the hardware design is not done. In fact, the

Hardware team may put things into the prototypes, like extra sensors, that are not intended to go into the final product at all.

Second, the hardware drops are not as frequent as the integration timeboxes. The assumption is that the software teams will test multiple drops on the same version of the hardware. If there's a serious problem with a prototype, the hardware team may be able to make a quick fix, but that's not the assumption.

The team plans out future slices using rolling-wave planning guided by a high-level plan to make sure they are on track to finish for an on-time launch. For small teams, this is enough.

Large Teams Pull Things Together with Integration Trains

Large, complex teams will need to work in a more structured way so they can spend their time on engineering rather than constantly re-planning. They will establish Integration Trains with rigor around what it takes to get on the train, when the train leaves and what happens to deliverables that miss the train.

Where to Begin with Agile for Physical Products

Software teams have one more luxury that physical product teams don't: They can start using Agile no matter where they are. If they are at the beginning, they can immediately build a backlog of user stories and figure out which user stories to develop in the first sprint. If the project has been running awhile, this will be more complicated but still possible and perhaps even more useful. The core of Agile is accessible to any software development team willing to make the leap.

Software teams can do this because their work has relatively low cost-of-change. In fact, in the worst-case scenario of a team using waterfall development — now in a death march due to rising system integration issues at the end — Agile may be the only way out. It will help the teams organize their work into smaller batches and prioritize that work so that the first working software can get out faster, then mature with rapid iteration.

Sometimes hardware teams also get so stuck that they need a radical reset. But for most teams, it can be more frustrating than helpful to introduce agile methods in middle to late development. They'll see what they should have done (and what their managers should have done) differently — where Key Decisions were made too early and with too little information — yet it will be too late to do anything except mitigate the risk and hope for the best.

It can be discouraging for a team to learn about Key Decisions and recognize that they and their leaders have already made some of these decisions — and deeply embedded them into their system designs and business plans — without the knowledge they needed to make confident decisions. For this reason, most of our clients opt to leave projects alone if they are already well into the Execution Phase of product development, unless they have no other choice.

Where is your best place to begin? Begin at the beginning, if possible, but allow for the possibility that some teams may need an Agile Reset. If your organization has tried to use Agile methods, and you now know why they're struggling, you may need an Agile Rescue Mission.

Begin at the Beginning If Possible

For most physical product development teams, the easiest place to start working differently is at the beginning. Teams have not yet made many decisions that could trigger loopbacks later. You get immediate benefit from asking the questions "What have we learned?" and "What do we need to learn next?" because these early phases are all about learning. They don't yet have the complexities of industrialization, and they don't need nearly as much hardware/software integration.

This means the place to start is with Rapid Learning Cycles. You can start Rapid Learning Cycles at the beginning of any phase centered on learning, usually one of the first three phases of a PDP. Teams starting at the Feasibility Phase may find that decisions made in earlier phases need to be revisited, but that's a lot better than discovering this problem later in development. At this early stage, problems are less overwhelming because they're easier to fix.

Not only does Rapid Learning Cycles provide structure to Early Development, it also helps the teams build skills in running programs using tools from queueing theory: small batches, timeboxes on a cadence, WIP limits, fast cycles of feedback.

They'll learn how much they can get done in a cycle, experience how Learning Cycle Events and Integration Events pull Knowledge Gaps and Key Decisions through the process, and learn how to prioritize and discover their team's norms for capturing knowledge, sharing it and revising the team's plans.

When your teams start using these practices and tools from the beginning, the Integration Trains have a smooth track to run on. But what if the team hasn't been using these tools, and now you can see that they are in trouble?

When a Waterfall Team Is in Trouble: The Agile Reset

Agile Resets are for teams that are struggling in the Execution Phase. They may already be behind schedule or have significant cost overruns. They may have encountered a serious reliability or manufacturability issue, or early users may have strongly disliked the way the product works. We can adapt the practices from earlier chapters to help these teams get unstuck.

First, they need a clear decision: Is this program worth continuing in its current form? We know that long, slow loopbacks burn a lot of time and money as teams frantically seek solutions to the problems that were uncovered. Yet the "sunk cost fallacy" encourages the organization to keep going in the hopes that the product can recoup at least some of the investment made. Sometimes the right decision is to kill it, or at least kill the current version of the product and start over, pulling in the pieces of the current version only as they make sense.

More often, the right answer is to keep going but change some things about how the team works. At an Agile Reset event, we assess the current state of the product and the program as a whole: What's actually done, which gaps and critical defects still remain to be closed, where does the system seem less stable and more error-prone, where are the major outstanding risks? Teams then build an Execution Cycle Plan and perhaps a slice-based integration plan.

The Execution Cycle Plan includes deliverables, defect fixes and perhaps even some Knowledge Gaps and Key Decisions (How will we reduce a component's cost by 15 percent?) to guide focused learning around major risks and gaps. The goal of the plan will be to get a MVP out as soon as possible. To accomplish this, some features may have to go, and some constraints may have to be relaxed.

Finally, teams in trouble need a firm launch date and a firm Go/No-Go decision date for that launch. They need the end to be in sight.

When Agile Software Methods Fail in Hardware: The Agile Rescue Mission

Since about 2015, Katherine has been called out several times a year on an "Agile Rescue Mission" to help a physical product group that got wrapped up in Agile Software Development practices. Sometimes the problems with exploding backlogs and project overhead became so severe that the Development teams had essentially ground to a halt.

We handle these missions a little differently than we handle individual teams that are stuck or organizations that are doing OK but want to get better, because these teams can be in some real trouble. We know we need to:

1. **Listen to them and affirm that their problems are real.** Agile coaches often tell these teams "You're just not doing Agile right" or "You just need to stick with it." They need to know that their experience is real, and that the side effects they're experiencing are shared with others who have tried the same thing.

2. **Remove the source of the problem.** To the extent possible, get the Agile Software Development people out of the room if they are too inflexible to be helpful. If you've given them this book, and they're open to the ideas, they may be able to stay — but only if they get themselves trained in these practices. Even if they're willing, they may have lost so much credibility that they need to be removed. Instead, redirect their energies towards working with firmware and software teams, for whom their knowledge and experience applies.

3. **Give teams permission to drop whatever's not working so they can use the right tools for the job.** Immediately tell teams they can stop doing anything that's not helpful. Daily standups are often the first thing to go.

4. **Restore visibility for the big picture and the long-term schedule.** Teams using Agile practices in the wrong context often lose sight of the big picture, and what they need to do to drive the project to completion because the backlogs don't handle dependencies well. They have to get their arms around the long-term plan and address any fallout from keeping this view hidden. These teams are also the most prone to having large backlogs that take hours to plan and re-plan. They need a good Level Zero plan for the entire project and a Level One plan for the current phase — probably a GANTT chart. In fact, they probably already have one stuck in a drawer where the Agile coach can't find it, but the entire team needs to see it and own it.

5. **Convert early teams to Rapid Learning Cycles immediately.**
   As soon as possible, transition teams early in development away
   from task-based sprints and towards knowledge-based Rapid
   Learning Cycles. Ensure that the team understands the flow of
   Key Decisions through their project, and that they are building
   the knowledge needed to make those decisions with confidence.

6. **Allow Execution Phase teams to go back to traditional project management until their project finishes.** Teams in Execution
   phases often benefit most by going backwards to traditional
   project management. This may seem counterintuitive since it may
   look like they're doing execution cycles on the surface. But as we
   mentioned above, teams often lose track of the dependencies and
   long-range plan when they lean too heavily into backlog management.

7. **Establish slice-based integration when it makes sense** — but
   not before. Teams that need to integrate with firmware and other
   software teams can benefit from slice-based integration, but that's
   not usually the first thing to introduce. The team needs the overall long-range plan first. Consider introducing slice-based integration (and other practices mentioned in Chapters Four, Five,
   and Six) on the *next* project, when the team has recovered and
   can make a fresh start.

The end state of the Agile Rescue Mission is that each team uses the
practices and tools that make the most sense for the phase of product
development that their project is in, without demanding conformity for
conformity's sake when teams just need to get unstuck.

Teams that have been asked to work with ill-fitting practices and tools
have been placed under a lot of pressure. The pressure only increases as
the backlogs blow up, project management overhead takes up more and
more time and the big picture gets harder and harder to see. To protect
themselves, they may have become disengaged or cynical. They may have

felt like they had to break the rules to do the right thing for their projects. For this reason, they may need to see that Rapid Learning Cycles, slice-based integration and other practices are working better for other teams before they are willing to try these things themselves.

With these teams, we tend to err on the side of giving them more freedom to choose their own ways of working, even when that looks like going backwards. They can keep the practices and tools that work and drop the ones that are not working. Meanwhile, we gently and carefully introduce new practices and tools to those Project Leaders who are willing to try.

Leaders sometimes worry if they'll lose face with their organizations if they abort their Agile transformation. Our experience has been the opposite. Teams appreciate their willingness to admit that Agile wasn't working and take steps to limit the damage. Team Leaders have said to me, "They finally listened to us." After a successful Agile Rescue Mission, teams can feel a tremendous sense of relief.

Your First Steps

The Agile for Physical Products system can help teams become faster, more flexible and more responsive — but not usually all at the same time.

If you have a waterfall team in trouble, the place to start is an Agile Reset. If you've been struggling with Agile Software Development, you need at least some of the elements of the Agile Rescue Mission. These will help alleviate the most immediate sources of pain.

What if you don't have that kind of burning platform? Choose your starting point by determining what your organization needs most from agile:

We need to accelerate product development with faster time-to-market.

If you're fairly confident that you have the right product programs, and you want them to get to market as fast as possible, the product program is the place to start.

Introduce Rapid Learning Cycles first at the Feasibility Phase of your PDP. This is the phase when your teams will make their most important decisions about the design direction for the products you have already planned, and where capturing knowledge has the most immediate value. Time spent here to build knowledge before committing to solutions pays off later with fewer problems to resolve during integration and industrialization.

Encourage teams to continue working in execution cycles as they move past this phase, and introduce slice-based integration plans if they make sense, when they make sense. Meanwhile, expand Rapid Learning Cycles to earlier phases of the PDP, all the way back to idea screening and Advanced R&D but only after the product teams are comfortable with agile.

We need to make better use of the people and money we have to invest in innovation to deliver the right products faster.
If you're not sure that you have the right products going into development, you've had a string of recent disappointments or product programs get stuck because the teams don't seem to have a good handle on customer or business value, we recommend starting in a different place.

The place to fix those problems is even earlier — in the earliest phases of the PDP or even the work done before a product enters the PDP. These are the phases that set the direction for the program, establishing the Core Hypothesis we described in Chapter Three.

Rapid Learning Cycles in these early phases help teams explore the opportunities before committing to a direction. They'll develop knowledge about the business case to help the leadership make better portfolio decisions, and they'll conduct technical assessments to get an early read on feasibility before committing to the program. They'll begin to build customer knowledge that will help the team make better early decisions on features, functionality and user experience.

All of this will help you make better decisions about the people and money you have to invest in product development programs so you can set them up for acceleration to get the right products faster.

We need to integrate more effectively with firmware and software to build products that bundle hardware with firmware, cloud software and apps.

A lot of hardware teams turn to agile because their firmware and software teams use a form of Agile Software Development. That's even more true with the advent of the IoT. Every year, more consumer products connect to cloud services via wireless networks, which then speak to consumers via apps.

Meanwhile, factory floors, distribution centers, maintenance hubs and even farming operations have an expanding array of connected devices. They collect data to feed into cloud services, analyze that data using artificial intelligence and then remotely change the behavior of the equipment. All of this means that hardware/software integration is a bigger challenge for more teams than it was even three years ago.

If you're new to this or struggling, slice-based integration plans will help make the integration process more visible and provide a smoother interface among the different groups that must work together if these products are going to work at all. You may even decide to experiment with the Integration Train from the beginning.

This will help solve your most immediate challenge first. After that, you can consider introducing the other practices as they make sense.

Agile Implementation is Fast, Flexible and Responsive

Agile for Physical Products will fundamentally change the way your teams organize their work, make decisions and collaborate with cross-functional partners. The more fully you adopt the practices, the more value you will receive from it.

Some organizations jump right into change with both feet, and others need more time to adjust. Some product development groups already deliver products at a pace that allows for rapid experimentation with agile practices, while others work on products that have more regulatory constraints or a more conservative market.

This is an area where we can go slower now to go faster later. We recommend piloting any practices you want to adopt on at least one team before deciding that this is the way all of your teams will work. After the first team is running, you can capitalize on enthusiasm to grow the agile practices organically as you build the structure and tools that will make this change more sustainable.

We have groups now that have been using Rapid Learning Cycles for over ten years, including the teams we described in Chapter One. Slice-based integration plans and Integration Trains are newer but still grounded in our real-world experience.

Not that long ago, those groups were where you are now. Today, they are faster, more flexible and more responsive — more agile. You can become more agile, too.

Afterword

In this book, we shared the journey we've been on since 2009. When the companies described in Chapter One began approaching Katherine to explore whether Agile Software Development practices could help them, she saw immediately that she needed Kathy's experience to figure out what that might mean. We've been learning together ever since.

The primary purpose of this book is to share the principles that build agility and the agile practices that best serve teams developing physical products. We wanted to explain why these practices are successful, when practices taken directly from Agile Software Development are often unsuccessful at helping teams become faster, more flexible and more responsive. If our explanations keep even one team from experiencing the ill effects of a misguided Agile implementation, we've done what we set out to do.

We learned that the Agile Software Development practices weren't helpful when they were applied directly. Fortunately, our clients stayed with us and committed themselves to a principles-driven path. The agile principles led to the breakthroughs that became the Rapid Learning Cycles framework and the rest of the Agile for Physical Products system we described here.

An Ongoing Stream of System Development

The practices that became the Rapid Learning Cycles framework were developed between 2010 and 2013, with major updates in 2015 and 2016, but Katherine doesn't consider the framework complete. Her team at the Rapid Learning Cycles Institute releases a new update to the framework at least once a year that captures what we've observed within our user community.

149

The long-term members of the Rapid Learning Cycles user community — the ones who use Rapid Learning Cycles on every product development program — have demonstrated how teams naturally carry over the structure of learning cycles while changing the content of the cycle. Chapter Four of this book is Katherine's first attempt to describe the common patterns in how they carry the learning cycles concept forward into execution. This part of the system is ripe for rapid evolution.

Starting in about 2015, Katherine began seeing the need for the Agile Rescue Missions she described in Chapter Seven, as a few popular books and articles started advocating for Agile Software Development practices outside of software. Once is bad luck, twice perhaps a coincidence, but the third time is a pattern. We learn as much or even more from the things that don't work. As long as people fall into the cognitive trap of the Law of the Instrument, we'll have opportunities to learn from misguided applications of Agile practices.

The work on slice-based integration plans and Integration Trains is newer, arising partly from a growing need for better hardware/software integration driven by IoT. Although the groundwork for this was put in place in the late 2000s, the full explanation has been pulled together more recently based on additional experience. As we begin to introduce these methods to more members of the Rapid Learning Cycles community and others interested in Agile for Physical Products, we expect to learn a lot more.

To Learn Fast, Share Early and Often

We also wrote this book to accelerate our learning by sharing what we've seen. We hope to spark more experimentation by thinking about other ways the agile principles could be applied in arenas outside of Agile

Software Development — without copying the rituals, ceremonies, practices and tools that are software-specific.

We've included here the practices that we think apply broadly to products that must go from small-scale proof of concept to production scale, whether the product is mechanical, biological or chemical. We already know that electrical engineers, packaging engineers and industrial designers can use some of these practices but may have better ones enabled by the technologies they use for their design work that lower cost-of-change for prototypes.

We believe there is potential for teams working in pharma, biotech, chemicals, agriculture, energy and specialty materials, among others, to apply queueing theory to the unique batches in their development processes, as we have done for hardware/software integration.

Additive manufacturing lurks on the horizon, promising to lower cost-of-change for some mechanical components the way that the internet brought down cost-of-change for software. We are still at the beginning of this new wave. While today it's only suited for products produced at low volumes, it won't end there. As the technology matures, it will become economically feasible to build more and more complex products this way, which will dramatically change the process of industrialization and supply chain management, creating new workflows with batches to optimize.

It's only been in the past fifteen years or so that physical product teams began to explore agile principles, and it's clear that our journey is only getting started.

Join Us on Our Journey

We hope that this book has inspired you to take action. When your own teams can be faster, more flexible and more responsive, they not only get products out faster with less frustration; they also build confidence in their ability to deliver innovative products — and you solidify your position as the innovation leader in your industry.

If you have already been exploring agile principles in physical product development, we'd like to connect with you, especially if you've come to different conclusions than we have. As visible experts in this field, people tend to come to us with the most difficult challenges; it could be that there are successes we haven't encountered because the people behind that success haven't asked for our help. We welcome the opportunity to see how others have responded to the same challenges.

If you're wondering where to start, the last page of the book offers some specific suggestions that we'll keep updated as they evolve. In the meantime, the Key Decision is a powerful concept that you can explore right away. Where do your teams have high impact/high unknown decisions? How can you help them make those decisions at the right time with the right people and the best available knowledge? If this is the only thing you do, your teams will be a bit faster, more flexible and more responsive — and excited about the possibility to go deeper.

For Further Reading

From Katherine Radeka:

High Velocity Innovation: How Innovators Get Their Best Ideas to Market Faster. Career Press, 2019. This book shares stories and best practices from companies that are using the Rapid Learning Cycles framework today, and shares what your organization can do once your teams are fast, flexible and responsive.

The Shortest Distance Between You and Your New Product, 2nd Edition. Chesapeake Research Press, 2017. This book describes the Rapid Learning Cycles framework in detail, and it's probably the book you should read next if you've decided to take your first steps.

Mastery of Innovation: A Lean Product Development Fieldbook. Productivity Press, 2012. This book includes the chapter that explains Suzanne van Egmond's Lean Scheduling system, which became multi-level planning in the Rapid Learning Cycles framework.

From Kathy Iberle:

Iberle, Kathleen. "Lean System Integration at HP." Proceedings of the Pacific Northwest Software Quality Conference 2010 (https://kiberle.com/wp-content/uploads/2016/01/2010-Lean-System-Integration-at-HP.pdf). This paper describes the work at HP in more detail. You may notice that, at the time, the term "sliver" was being used instead of "slice."

Iberle, Kathy. "Fix Your Agile Project by Taking a Systems View." Agile Connection, July 24, 2013. Downloaded 12/22/2021. https://www. agileconnection.com/article/fix-your-agile-project-taking-systems-view. This article goes more deeply into the history behind the adoption of agile methods in software over the years, and Kathy's realization that queueing theory principles were driving Agile Software Development.

Kathy has written about batches and flow management in other contexts:

Software tests: "Lean in the Test Lab." Proceedings of the Pacific Northwest Software Quality Conference 2013 (https://kiberle.com/wp-content/uploads/2016/01/2013-Lean-in-The-Test-Lab-1.pdf).

Improvement projects: "Introducing Fast Flexible Flow at HP." Lean Product and Process Development Exchange 2012 (https://kiberle. com/wp-content/uploads/2016/01/2012-Introducing-Fast-Flexible-Flow-at-HP.pdf).

Small tool development projects: "Kanban: What Is It and Why Should I Care?" (with Landon Reese). Proceedings of the Pacific Northwest Software Quality Conference 2011 (https://kiberle.com/wp-content/uploads/2016/01/2011-Kanban-at-HP.pdf).

Other Works:

Chapter Two

Reinertsen, Donald G. *Principles of Product Development Flow: Second-Generation Lean Product Development.* Celeritas Publishing, Redondo Beach, California, 2009. A treasure trove of theory and practical application. Reinertsen shows you how to see the batches and queues throughout your organization, and what can be done to accelerate flow.

NOTE: Chapter Two mentions that Kathy read Reinertsen's *Managing the Design Factory*. When *Principles of Product Development Flow* was published shortly thereafter, the more recent book quickly became her top recommendation.

Chapters 3 and 4

Poppendieck, Mary; Poppendieck, Tom. *Lean Software Development: An Agile Toolkit*. Addison-Wesley, 2003. Mary Poppendieck was one of the early people to recognize that Lean Manufacturing and Agile Software Development were both applications of queueing theory. At first, people tried to apply Lean Manufacturing ideas to software, another instance of the Law of the Instrument we described in the Introduction. Poppendieck started here too but quickly realized that it wasn't sufficient. By the end of the 2010s, many authors were applying queueing theory ideas directly to software development, often aided by Reinertsen's *Principles of Product Development Flow*.

Chapter 4

Smith, Preston G. *Flexible Product Development: Agile Hardware Development to Liberate Innovation*, 2007, 2018. This book contains many more ideas on how to speed up various aspects of hardware development by using techniques borrowed or adapted from agile.

Gruver, Gary. Young, Mike. Fulghum, Pat. *A Practical Approach to Large-Scale Agile Development: How HP Transformed LaserJet FutureSmart Firmware*. Addison-Wesley, 2013. The use of emulators and simulators to obtain earlier feedback is discussed in Chapter Six of this book. It's also a good look at how firmware teams commonly implement Agile Software Development methods.

Chapter 5 and 6

Wake, Bill. "INVEST in Good Stories, and SMART Tasks" (https://xp123.com/articles/invest-in-good-stories-and-smart-tasks/). Posted August 17, 2003. Downloaded November 15, 2021. Bill Wake describes slicing vertically through the layers to provide the customer with "the essence of the whole cake." In queueing theory terms, this vertical slice is a batch that delivers value to the customer.

Rothman, Johanna. *Create Your Successful Agile Project: Collaborate, Measure, Estimate, Deliver.* Pragmatic Bookshelf, Raleigh, North Carolina, 2017. In the chapter "Teams Deliver Features," you'll see a software-centric description of most of the tools we've discussed in Chapters Four through Six. If you think of user stories as batches, and epics as a batch of small batches, you'll see this book describing how these batches deliver value to end users and to the organization, why these batches should slice across the architecture, the "walking skeleton" and how to use multi-level planning and rolling-wave roadmaps. Software teams have been using these tools for over twenty years, so they have gotten quite good at it!

Rothman, Johanna. *Agile and Lean Program Management: Scaling Collaboration Across the Organization.* Practical Ink, Arlington, Massachusetts, 2016. The "agile roadmap" described in the chapter "Integrating Hardware into Your Program" is similar to the slice method we describe.

Acknowledgements

Kathy and Katherine first met at HP in 1999 and became fast friends and collaboration partners. This book is the latest fruit of a productive partnership that has spanned more than twenty years, four companies and more days spent co-leading client workshops than either would care to count.

This book would not have been possible without the people there at the beginning of this journey. Roger Johnson, Christian Gianni, Jeff Williams, Prakash Jayarama, Sugosh Venkataraman, Kurt Heidmann, Tim Schipper, Wendy Hoerner, Mattias Hansson, Carsten Lauridsen, Lone Baunsgaard, Luise Erlandsen, Anders Ohmann and many others worked with Katherine to test her ideas during the early parts of the story told in Chapter One.

Kathy would like to thank Bret Dodd for opening her eyes to queueing theory and its uses, Ann Dunkin for her constant encouragement to think bigger, Dr. Cem Kaner for teaching Kathy so much about teaching, her colleagues at HP McMinnville for the opportunity to see all aspects of product development up close, Adam Light and the Agile Fluency community of Portland for their interesting and challenging conversations and all her HP colleagues involved in the stories we've told for their inventive work, willingness to try new things and unflagging team spirit.

Katherine and Kathy jointly thank Tine Jørgensen and Anette Sams Nielsen for the opportunity to engage with their research labs at the start of this journey. Insights from Emily Johnston, Matt Phillips, Jen Webb, Chris Harvey, Jenn Smith, Ryan Fitzgerald, Tony Macaluso, Chris Shuldiner, Todd Porter, Karen Cavoretto and Chris Godfrey have informed our most recent work.

Our early readers gave us valuable feedback to make this a better book. We especially thank Johanna Rothman who went above and beyond to make sure that we understood the latest developments in Agile Software Development.

The RLCI staff got this book done. Teri O'Hara drove the book the rest of the way from Written to Published. Shivaun Black kept all our systems running. Our network of Rapid Learning Cycles Certified® Affiliates provided insights as the manuscript developed, especially Brian Cohn, Edwin Schumacher, Lizet Bary and Fernanda Torre.

Katherine's dedication to making a difference with her work is fostered by her friendships with Heidi Franklin, Jeanette Grimaldi, Janet Buck, Kris Young, Marty Sturdivant, Pat Mickiewicz, Mary Jo Chaves, Larry Peacock, Eileen Parfrey, Terry Cappiello, Ben Coombs, Emmett Wheatfall, Nancy Pyburn, Linda Smith, Christine Peters, Tom Dudley and Ed Wales.

Finally, Katherine and Kathy want to thank our husbands, Gene Radeka and Tom Iberle, for sharing this journey with us, for their endless patience with the numerous schedule changes, and for supporting us every day in so many ways, large and small.

Index

About the Authors

KATHERINE RADEKA is the founder and executive director of the Rapid Learning Cycles Institute and supports a growing global community of Rapid Learning Cycles Certified® Professionals who are actively using the framework to get their best ideas to market faster.

She has worked with companies on every continent except Antarctica, and in industries from aerospace to medical devices and pharmaceuticals to consumer electronics and alternative energy. In 2021, she launched the Accelerate Net Zero project to share her expertise with startups and early-stage innovation programs working on climate tech.

In 2015, Katherine published the 1st edition of *The Shortest Distance Between You and Your New Product*. In 2012, she published the Shingo Research Award winning book *The Mastery of Innovation*, based upon her research into Lean methods for product development.

Katherine has climbed seven of the tallest peaks in the Cascade Mountains and spent ten days alone on the Pacific Crest Trail — until an encounter with a bear convinced her that she needed a change in strategic direction.

KATHY IBERLE has been working in Lean and Agile product development for over twenty years, using cutting-edge methods to help strengthen development and make mixed hardware/software projects run more smoothly. She's worked with many types of products — printers, medical instruments, electronic instruments, and website apps – and in a variety of roles from developer to quality assurance expert to agile adoption leader.

Since 1998, Kathy has been developing professional training courses — first for her fellow engineers at HP and later for a wider audience as a consultant. Recently she began authoring courses for Rapid Learning Cycles Certified® Professionals seeking the advanced Rapid Learning Cycles certification that will give them the skills to adapt the Rapid Learning Cycles framework for their organizations and train others how to use it.

Kathy was an early collaboration partner whose work directly contributed to the development of the Rapid Learning Cycles framework as we know it today. She was the first Rapid Learning Cycles Certified® Advisor fully licensed to share the Rapid Learning Cycles framework with others, and she is still the person Katherine calls on first to help with RLCI's toughest client challenges.